CW01574497

To Ann &

a longstanding friend,

With love & hugs,

from Di x.

Home at Last

Home at Last

Di Shouls

SilverWood

Published in hardback 2011 by SilverWood Books, Bristol, BS1 4HJ
www.silverwoodbooks.co.uk

Copyright © Di Shouls 2011

The right of Di Shouls to be identified as the author of this work
has been asserted by her in accordance with the Copyright,
Designs and Patents Act 1988.

All rights reserved. No part of this publication may be reproduced,
stored in a retrieval system, or transmitted in any form or by any means,
electronic, mechanical, photocopying, recording or otherwise,
without prior permission of the copyright holder.

ISBN 978-1-906236-68-7

British Library Cataloguing in Publication Data
A CIP catalogue record for this book is available from the British Library

Set in Palatino by SilverWood Books
Printed in England on paper certified as being from responsible sources

Foreword

This is a true story set in England in the 1960s, when we were all very young. It draws from real-life diaries of the time (although most of the names have been changed) and tells of the long search for a child who has no family – the modern orphan – and the experiences and heartaches involved. The final climax comes four years later, when the child's legal adoption is granted, and he is given his heritage for the first time. A home and family that is truly his.

Di Shouls

Acknowledgements

This book is written with immense thanks to Matthew, my husband, without whom there would be no story, and to my five irrepressible children. To the Voluntary Christian charity who cared for Jeremy until he came to us, and to my wonderful Mother and Father who have shown such kindness to us all. To Bridget, who typed relentlessly for me. And to God whose strength I seemed to constantly need!

May I also thank the many friends and acquaintances who have unwittingly given me much of the material for the story.

The names have of course, been changed throughout the book.

Room For One More?

1

For a long time now, the yearning had been there. I just longed for a big family. And at last, after eight years of being married to Matthew, we had three daughters and one son. Jackie was seven, a sweet creative little girl, Peter five, Rosemary three, and little Louise, just six months. I had to concede that this was a start, anyway. The children were a joy, and we wanted so very much to share our very great happiness. We had a lot of fun and such good times together.

I very much wanted to bring into our family some children, one to start with, who were deprived of a normal family life, and the support of a Mummy and Daddy who cared. As a family we took our responsibilities very seriously, and I felt certain that if we tried long enough, we could find the right child to come and be our child.

We, or rather I, at this stage, had thought about this a great deal. Could we do this thing? Would we really have the strength to see it through? How would the children deal with the situation? Over and again I examined it all from every standpoint. But one thing still stood out clearly. Here were we, our home, our family. We had given ourselves to God, in prayer, and here was one thing we could do, and would like to do, for Him.

Perhaps I lacked faith, but one thing worried me more than anything else. I found other people being too hard-up, a sordid, distressing thing, and here were we with our pennies already stretched to the very limit each month. Even though Matthew was earning to me an enormous amount of money, we only just made ends meet, and knew all the tricks of the trade – economy meals, passed-on clothes, trousers with more patch than trouser (our Granny is just a miracle at mending), cheap holidays, long walks in the country, and of course, homemade everything. I knew that we would give our new little child ourselves, our home, everything that he needs, but I realised rather sadly that this work which I so desperately wanted to do, must not cost us any money.

The Local Authorities and Voluntary Societies all paid very little each week for a child to be fostered out permanently into a normal family, and I knew that this would not cover the costs involved in taking a child.

But as I looked at our own radiant children, their eyes shining, I just knew. We must try to find a child, the first must be a boy for Peter's sake, and then try to persuade the Authority to make an adequate allowance for him.

We so desperately believed that every little life is so immensely precious, and longed to share ourselves, our homes, and our love with another little person, that in this normal environment we may help a whole man emerge, a person able to find his own independence and interdependence in the world, and, we pray, able to find God. We had thought so many thoughts, and wondered so many things. Could we, we asked ourselves, keep alight, or rekindle that vital spark in a child which sometimes dies when a child is in care, is cared for, but not loved in a belonging sort of way? I think each one of us needs to belong, to be needed by someone. We needed another little son. Somewhere, surely, was a little son needing us.

2

Advertisements frequently appeared in newspapers and magazines on behalf of children needing a home. So began an enlightening task.

Above: Peter, Rosemary and Jackie

Right: Louise

I wrote enquiring about these children and the more letters I wrote, the more I became aware of the problems of the children and the society in which we live. Our England, where our lack of compassion, and our laws are throwing these children into an environment from which many will not, cannot, emerge triumphant.

If only everyone of us who loves God and follows Jesus, however haltingly, were to really examine our attitudes and see what is really right, not conventional, surely a more humble kindness would arise, which could see every other person as our brother, in the sense that we are all God's children. Then when one of us falls, we might be able to involve, rather than insulate ourselves. This all applies also, of course, to those of us who are not convinced as Christians, but who simply love people for themselves.

Our society has condemned a lot of people by lack of kindness, and by priorities being in the wrong order. Could we not give more to help to the unmarried Mother who wants to keep her baby, and love her as we love a married Mother, I mean with practical love? Then the divorced Mothers who may frequently be depending in practice just on Social Security. Could not the people, in fact all of us with successful marriages, be humbly thrilled with our good fortune, and our husbands, and more willing to open our eyes to see where help is needed?

Could we, as a nation, make it more feasible for all those of us who love children and people, to take the needy and neglected children into our hearts and homes, by making this into a job of work? Is it not possible to pay the full cost of keeping a child to a family who wants to do this work?

One advertisement in particular I followed up offering a home for a baby boy. It appeared that this little soul had been found abandoned in a telephone kiosk, and there had been no success in finding any relatives. Oh, how I wanted this baby! I used to lie awake at night thinking of him, wondering if they had time in the nursery to cuddle him and make the dotty noise that makes babies laugh. Already I loved this child, in the same way, I suppose, as I did the children before they were born, and I prayed desperately in the way one does when things are important to one. I did so want him in our family, before he got too terribly hurt. I knew that to take only one child is but a drop in the ocean, but if we could save this one little person from being wretched, I would be so glad.

Sometimes, I would look at our youngest baby daughter, Louise, lying in her cot and see her beaming face. "To be wanted by no one." Can there be anything worse?

So now we had only to persuade the Children's Officer that we were the right people for this child. Letters between us took so long. The weeks went by, still he had no Mummy and Daddy and here we were waiting for him.

> ***Challenge***
> *Can you provide a home for a physically handicapped girl, a coloured girl, a deaf girl, a backward boy or a baby boy? All these children need the love and security of a good home. The physically handicapped girl and the deaf girl need a home in the Wokingham area so that their education can continue without interruption.*
>
> *Anyone who can respond to the challenge that the long term care of one of these children would offer is invited to apply for further details to the County Children's Officer, 35 Bath Road, Reading.*

3

At last we decided that we must make a definite move about this babe and we went over to Reading, to keep an appointment with the Children's Department. We were assigned to see the Assistant

Children's Officer, who, in this area, was responsible for finding foster parents and placing the children with them. We were terribly excited, certain as we were by now that, with an interview almost taking place, we were at least high on the list as a new Mummy and Daddy for the babe. It felt the same as if we were about to have born to us another "natural" baby. Those precious moments were ahead when, very humbly, we would introduce ourselves to this little person who was being entrusted to our care. Would he respond to us when I held him in my arms, or would we gradually have to win our way into his affection?

We arrived at the right department on the dot of eleven, after depositing the two youngest children with neighbours and getting Jackie and Peter off to school. It was a lovely bright day, and the journey to Reading took just two hours. What a treat it always was to contrive to get off entirely on our own. Then there was a chance, at least, of being able to think an intelligent and uninterrupted thought!

The building was impressive. Brand new and well fitted out, but I wondered why these administrative offices had to be built in the dense centre of town.

Mr. Gregg came in and for the first time, we met. It turned out in fact, that all our correspondence had been with Mr. Gregg, though there had been no clue about this. Why, I wondered, could not letters be signed with the writer's own name so that one knew who one was really dealing with? Our baby, he told us, so casually, had been placed with another family and the finalities would be discussed that afternoon.

My disappointment was enormous, for in our hearts and the hearts of the children, there was already a place for this little boy. I was terribly sad. Of course, I was glad that they had found what they felt was a good family for this little boy, but very disappointed that this wonderful thing had not materialised for us. I loved this child. They had called him Paul at the nursery, he was six months old, and

I just hoped that he would be happy, and would have all the help he needed through his difficulties.

We talked for over an hour about all aspects of the children in care and went through lists of children still needing a family. There were two more baby boys, brain damaged babies, but I felt that at this stage our greatest contribution would be with normal children. If only it were two years hence, I thought, for they had two little sisters, aged two and four years old, needing a family. But I still felt that in our family, the first child should be a boy. These children tread a difficult path, and we wanted to give them the very best chance we could. A ready made big brother would be a great asset to a boy and Peter was a sweet boy with a gentle nature. Perhaps when we found our boy, we could dream again of more little girls.

I wept as soon as I got outside, but really only with selfish disappointment. In spite of an apparently fruitless journey, I felt we had learnt a lot.

4

Some years ago, the newspapers publicised two tragic happenings among children whose normal family life had been disturbed. In Dorset, a little boy of twelve, in the care of a foster home, was assaulted for three years by a lodger living in the same house. (It seems that quite often foster parents must take in other paying guests, in order to actually pay for the cost of their foster child. The boarding out rates do not cover the cost.)

The other incident was even more disturbing to my mind. An illegitimate baby was placed by the mother in the hands of an adoption society, who found what seemed to be an ideal family for him. As the adoption order came up, the blood father appeared and asked for the child, whom he had never seen. He and his second wife were 48 years old. The judge ruled that the baby, a little boy of nineteen months, should be taken from the adopting parents, whom he loved and knew, to go to the father, who to date had but sired him.

What sobering and tragic situations.

5

Saturday dawned a marvellous day. The sky was quite clear and though it was still only the first week in March, the sun shone and it was warm. Matthew started once again on the mammoth task of levelling the garden ready for us to rotivate and sow the grass seed. But as we stood idling about in the sunshine, the children came up with a lovely idea – what a gorgeous day to go to the coast. It did not take us very long to load up the picnic basket, an unsophisticated bright plastic laundry basket, with bread and butter, sausages for frying, saucepans, milk, squash and a giant tin of fruit for afters. We hoped that we could make a fire on the beach and so we took one fire lighter and some matches. And, of course, a series of sundry objects, dry socks for everyone, nappies, bottles of milk and a tin of baby food for Louise.

Soon we were ready – it is always a surprise how quick we can be when we all want to do something very much! Jackie felt a bit glum at the prospect of being stuck on the car journey, but we were soon there, and no sickness. We decided to make for Seaford, in Sussex, to start with, and then drive later to Newhaven, where we knew that there were boats.

The beach at Seaford was so inviting and at this time of year quite deserted. The beach was a fine shingle, but we were all wearing boots, so the stones did not bother us. With the children helping we soon unloaded, and found our spot on the beach and laid out our camp – a huge plastic tablecloth covered with a large rug. The children were so happy, Louise cosily snuggled in the carry-cot on wheels, and Jackie, Peter and Rosemary digging and making dams. There were several small sailing crafts out to sea and one speedboat skimming about, and to our joy the sun was still out, and no wind. Matthew and I gathered a lot of driftwood together in a sheltered spot near the breakwater. There was plenty of it and as it was dry, our fire was soon blazing. Fried sausages – how good they taste when you feel hungry. Crusts torn off the loaf and buttered, then tinned fruit. Coffee was on the menu for Matthew and me but when we tasted it, our enthusiasm waned. It had an acid smoky taste, boiled and only then did we discover that the sugar was still sitting in the kitchen at home! Horrible and quite undrinkable. But the children were happy with their squash.

By now the children had wet boots and trousers, so on the finer shingle, they were able to run barefoot. The tar was a real nuisance, lying about in thick tantalising lumps which just could not be avoided completely, and soon we had our tally of tar on the clothes. But nearer the sea it was better and we escaped it then. Jackie and Peter undressed and tried to swim but it was really frr-eee-zing cold and they could not go in. I did not notice Matthew or I making any conspicuous efforts to lead the way though!

Quite early in the afternoon the warmth began to fade, so we packed up and went to neighbouring Newhaven, just in time to see the ferry coming in from France. Beside the harbour is a small yacht marina. It was a joy to see all the small craft lying in their moorings. Some were being painted and cleaned up for the first outings around Easter I suppose, and it was good to walk around watching all the activity.

Sunday was a memorable day too, but in a different way. Matthew was gardening again, or should it be just called labouring at this stage, and the children and some friends were playing outside with the toys. Suddenly we sensed something was amiss.

Next to our garden was a rough copse which belonged to another house, and in this were some huge and beautiful pine trees. We looked round for all the children. Peter was nowhere to be seen, but it soon became apparent from the other children that he was in one of the trees. But still we could not see him. He was right up near the very top, over fifty feet up. He was quite happy, but we were terrified. There were so many dead branches in this tree, and it is difficult to distinguish between alive and dead from inside the tree. If he slipped from this height – the thought was hardly bearable. I rang 999, hoping that this adventurous little lamb would sit tight and quietly until the fire engine ladder could reach him from the nearby road, and lift him safely down. Matthew stood underneath and gently encouraged him to climb carefully down, hoping that he would not tire or slip or choose a very dead branch.

The speed of the emergency service impressed us tremendously, and it was an enormous relief to feel the whole operation slide meticulously into action. Within two minutes they were out and on their way. How grateful one is, when a real emergency does occur, to know that efficient help is available.

Our boy in fact got himself down safely and the fire brigade recalled by radio. How deeply glad and thankful we were. And how aged we both felt when it was over. As we looked at his young slight body, we felt we would never again take him for granted.

Mr. Barber came for lunch that day. It was always a joy to have him. He was very old and gentle, wise and fun and so good for us all. In his younger days, he was a London Cabby, and of course has a wealth of true stories to call on, and a gorgeous smile. As a treat he had brought over for us a bottle of his home-made rice wine. Saki, it is called. To give a little flavour, he added an orange and a lemon, when making it, and it was delicious and very clear. Nicknamed "Ali", Mr. Barber always had a tin full of the juiciest toffees, and drew beautifully to delight the children. It was in knowing Ali that I hoped the children would learn a little of the needs of old people. The young and the old have so much to give to each other, and certainly we all feel the richer for having been in Mr. Barber's company. He loved to read his bible and so obviously looked forward to the future with real joy.

Matthew took Jackie and Peter to the Swimming Bath this afternoon. Such a radiant little Jackie came home. At last she had swum on her very own, just about two yards of dog paddle, but a start. How pleased we all felt for her.

6

These were such happy days. We had all now settled completely in our Sussex home and the children were radiant. The house and work were easier to do as at last Matthew had given me a small back terrace for the washing lines and had started to transform yet another dreary clay patch into a neat cheerful lawn.

The letters of reference for the County Council Children's Department had been written by our two friends who had agreed to do this, and what a support we found them to be. I still wondered if our dream could possibly materialise. A venture of faith, one of those friends called it!

We then made a formal application to East Sussex County Council to become Foster Parents. Still we felt that our greatest contribution could be with children whose families had broken down completely and who would be permanent.

We received two visits from the Area Children's Officer and felt somewhat despondent after these. It seemed to me that we had not done at all well, the children fought all the time, and it appeared to me that I had said all the wrong things, but things which nevertheless I felt needed saying. We filled in the form with one omission, stating the husband's income. This we felt was our private matter. Matthew had a good job at the time, was doing well and we were buying our own house. These we felt were the only relevant factors. Even if these things were not true, it would have made no difference to us as parents.

One other bit of impertinence I felt was a typed postscript stating that WE would be charged with any fee presented by our doctor, when asked by the Children's Officer about our health!

It was the wettest April since 1930 so we heard, and with three inches in four days, our poor lawn had well nigh been washed away. Poor Matthew – after all his hard work. I felt sure that the shimmer of green that I saw must be moss or mildew.

We decided to visit Croydon, really to inspect camping equipment at an exhibition there. One day we would like to get kitted up for camping but we would have to save up a while for those things, or perhaps later, we could acquire a second hand outfit. So many folk have apparently bought everything, only to find that after one attempt, it was a dismal failure, and not quite the holiday bliss which they expected.

The rain continued, so we lunched in one of the stores. We were there early, just after twelve o'clock and they were so kind, with high chairs for Louise and Rosemary, and one adult portion of lunch divided between them. One so appreciates kindness, for it can be so harrowing with the whole family out, when there is non-co-operation!

Afterwards, we were all tired and so made a visit to the animal shop in Kennards Arcade. In the window, we all noticed the most lovely sand-coloured guinea pig, and by common assent, he became ours plus 10p worth of hay, and a bag of food pellets and cereals, placed in a cardboard box and carried with such tenderness.

It was nice to have a little animal again, and all the children's grumbles had gone with this little chap's arrival. That afternoon, Matthew made a cage, a fine stout one of wood, which would be the guinea pig's home. He was honey-coloured, with white patches and had fine soft fur. We just called him "Guinea". The next morning, he delighted us all by nibbling a piece of apple, and then all Peter's breakfast Weetabix. Of course, he spent a great deal of time being carried around the house and left his little trail of droppings. I insisted that these be cleared up and thrown away. (Rosemary called them "snowdrops".)

The children's humour was so blissful and so unconscious at that age, and, of course, there was plenty of it. In fact, I sometimes wondered why they didn't make a film about us all. Like the time one Christmas when Jackie made Christmas cards for the children. One card was so beautifully written –

"To dear Louise from Jackie M."

We always had Jackie M – just to distinguish her from the other Jackies, no doubt.

Our attendance at Church those days was somewhat better. Very early on, we decided to worship as a family and take the children with us to Church occasionally. This gave us some harrowing experiences, as our children were not the sort that would sit quietly for one hour. But this Church gave us such a welcome and were so kind to the children when we did unloads ourselves on them.

One amusing time I had with Rosemary – it was Communion. Quietly we went up to the communion rail. I kneeled down, with Rosemary standing beside me. After a moment's prayer, I thought I had better just check on her. There she was swinging gaily on the brass rail – so happily, just a perfect trip-up for the priest as he walked along serving the sacraments.

7

One day, Matthew came home with a second hand typewriter and I became fired with enthusiasm. I was under the illusion that I could become a more efficient correspondent using a typewriter, but how does one avoid becoming a *press-press-erase-brrrr-ding* type of personality in the meanwhile!

An amusing incident occurred when we were in the nearby park – the children were swinging and sliding and the mothers were chatting. One little girlie went off on the long trek over the field to the toilets, but was back a little too soon. She could not go in because it said "vacant" on the door!

Matthew did a wonderful job in our garden and to our delight, we at last had grass back and front again. After the everlasting mud, it looked so nice and it was really green! There were trees in and surrounding the garden and two were strong enough for the children to climb. As the weather improved, we were able to have picnics outside and the big children would sit in the tree eating their snacks. Spaghetti was a favourite and long strands would come floating down, I rather fancy on purpose.

Jackie and Peter went back happily to school that term. Peter, as always, was glad to be back among the boys, and Jackie, I knew, felt a little sorry to have to be away from her Mum all day! The previous term, she had trouble with bullying from a child, which started to wear her down and she got so very crabby at home and quite beastly. It was our first experience of bullying, so first Jackie and I prayed together about it, knowing that if we put it into God's hands, He certainly would have some ideas for the solution. After that we made great fun about it all, suggesting awful jokes that we might play on the child, and laughing a great deal to try to keep it all in perspective. But still it went on, so that some days, she came home weary with it all. Without Jackie knowing, Matthew saw her teacher and, as we expected, she already knew about it and we left her to deal with it. Rather as we had surmised, the little "bully" was having problems of her own. Her parents were divorced but she had a splendid mother who really loved and cared for the child. We left it there, and gradually it was obvious that things were getting better, and then, to my surprise, the following term she was placed next to this child in class. All was completely well and all the unpleasantness forgotten. What clever psychology!

It seemed hard to believe but we were at last actually getting a full night's sleep, after simply years of getting up for somebody, so while the going was good, we thought we had better make the most of it. It was so nice to wake up in the morning not feeling tired.

The mini-skirt phase had arrived and to our delight, a tiny knitted red skirt arrived from our dear friend in Devon, in a parcel of little old clothes. It looked exquisite on Rosemary, yanked right up with braces.

I had tried the typing! It was surprising how very few letters need to be misplaced for the whole thing to "lookee very Chinesee".

Great excitement – after long searches in the "For Sale" column of our local paper, we at last saw what looked like our piano. "Good condition, £5". We phoned the family and arranged to go over the following evening. A delightful couple had kept it until we arrived and we were only too pleased to try it and hand over our cheque. It was delivered in a couple of days time and, soon after it arrived, a friend called to see us and, unlike Matthew and me, she could really play. It was lovely to hear our new acquisition come to life, and to me it sounded quite magnificent. She was so polite about it!

If any of our little people showed any real talent when they were older, we could then buy a really good piano for them. Our total musical talent ended with chopsticks played by me, Matthew, Jackie and Peter, and the first few bars of "Minuet in G", my piece de resistance! And of course, great concoctions by everyone. Even Louise would stand and stretch up her tiny fingers to produce a few notes.

She was such a joy. After the few days of spring sunshine, her skin was a beautiful brown and she looked so well. She was crawling all around, standing a little and eating well. Even her cod liver oil and rosehip syrup went down well, giving her the essential vitamins D and C. She "talked" endlessly to us all and to top her repertoire was that ever-appealing "Mum-Mum" and "Dad-Dad". The other children were very sweet with her and took great pleasure in making her chuckle.

We then had a letter from the Children's Department to say that we had been formally accepted as Foster Parents. Now we must wait until the time was right and our first little orpheline would come into our family.

Jackie's headmistress used to write a letter each holiday to the parents, with all the news of the previous term, points on which she needed our co-operation and information about the next term's prospects. This term, she discovered among her children a scheme for sending up recipes made with Shredded Wheat. Each child got a shilling back in return. The girl whose recipe suggested "Shredded Wheat and Oysters" was considered the winner!

8

One morning, a telephone call took us by surprise. It was the Children's Department and they wanted me to take a baby who might be coming into care, if they could find a suitable foster home. He was a little boy of twenty months, also called Peter, who was mentally retarded, and showed no interest in anything. He had only progressed to the age of a normal baby of about eight months, and they felt that this might have an emotional cause, perhaps due to knowing that he was not loved and wanted. They were undecided what to do with him as putting him into a nursery would achieve very little, as this child was too good and would simply get overlooked in a crowd. Above all, he needed the love and constant stimulation that occurs naturally in a normal family, in order to find out if it was just a great sadness in him that made it impossible for him to develop normally.

His mother was still looking after him but, at this stage, wanted him adopted. There was another little girl in the family whom the mother loved, and there was no effective father for the family, but a granny, who felt it in the child's best interest for the little boy to go away.

How could a child like this come into our family? His name was the same as our only son. He fitted in between Rosemary and Louise.

I was told that I could not see him before taking him, and that it was to be a permanent fostering. Thoughts started running around my head, sad thoughts, though as so many people were involved, I did try to think objectively.

My first aim and object with any young child would be to encourage a strong attachment with us and the children. Supposing after a while with us this attachment was formed and he recognised us as the strong support parents should be, but failed, and this was a strong possibility, to develop mentally. Surely to take such a child away from us then would really be worse than terrible. And then, at any time, his mother could ask for him back. Could he stand another upheaval without his little heart breaking completely.

The other thing which interested me. Already I could see that Foster Children lack status in this country. As was constantly emphasised, Foster Children are different, but was this in fact due to their enormous problems, or were the constant visits of the Child Care Officers in itself a disturbing factor? Was it not possible to choose Foster Parents with the care of choosing Marriage Guidance Counsellors or the clergy, pay them a realistic amount for the children, and then leave them to get on with the work with a minimum of supervision?

In a normal family, anyone visiting would do so only on terms of a friend. Could we adjust, I wondered, to visits from "The Authorities"? It also seems quite wrong to talk about the children in front of them. Talk we must all do, but never in the hearing of any of them.

All this gradually drew me to the conclusion that, at the moment, any children we had should be truly available for adoption, so that if we found that the Authorities in fact did disrupt the family more than was good for our own children, we could adopt, and become a self-contained unit once again.

I knew all this did not solve the problem. So often fostering is making the best of a very bad job, but nevertheless, we must do the best that we can in the light of all the knowledge that we have.

With our accommodation very limited and no absolute certainty of being able to get a bigger house, there were a lot of practical factors to weigh up.

So, with very real sadness, and a deep gloom in my heart, I said that we would not have this baby.

Later, they came again, to ask if I would take two children whose parents had no home, but again I declined, feeling very strongly, as so many people do, that this is one time when children should not be taken into care and separated from their parents. Somehow the whole family must be helped to stay together and I did not want to be a party to a situation I so heartily disagreed with.

I noticed that both these two placements were ones in which the foster children would have been placed in among our natural children, which I am told is considered to be unwise!

The Arrival Of Amimbola

1

This chapter in our life started in a very unexpected way. My husband Matthew had been having a spell of bad breath and so, after all else had failed, I persuaded him to visit the doctor. To my surprise and horror, an appointment was made for him to see the Specialist at our local hospital the very next week. A genito-urinary specialist! Even my wildest imagination failed to see any connection between that department of his anatomy and bad breath!

Such an urgent appointment. The Doctor had found an ominous looking lump on one of his private parts. Poor Matthew was so scared and felt that for him this was just the beginning of the end. He daily became greyer, and spoke in the hushed tones of a man with just a matter of a few more weeks to live. I was worried, but not in the same way, as I have made it a matter of policy not to really worry until we are certain that there is need to. It might turn out to be nothing. He had looked so tremendously well that it was difficult for me to believe that anything was seriously wrong.

His admission was arranged for the following week. It was Matthew's first experience in hospital and I went with him. He was so frightened when we arrived, and completely cold, with nerves, I suppose. This all amused me slightly, for having worked professionally in hospitals for years, I knew it would not be quite as bad as he feared, but of course, he could not be reassured.

The operation went perfectly and there were no complications.

It was just a cyst. Matthew read his New English Bible ferociously – even though we are practising Christians, I have never seen him quite so devoted before, and he made a normal and very loving recovery. There are certain times like this when men are so priceless. I had visited him twice each day, with all the arranging of baby minders for the children that this involved, apart from everything else, and as I sat beside his bed, really loving to be together again, I was asked "Had I been out at all today?"

My mother was terribly funny over all this, and could not take it too seriously. She never had been too keen on these bigger, albeit planned families, and wondered if, while the Surgeon was busy with Matthew's never-never regions, could he not just snip a little something, and so ensure that no more little grandchildren came along, from us at any rate!

One of the nurses looking after Matthew was a warm-hearted, lovely girl from Nigeria, Matthew's special nurse. He found her so gentle and one day remarked that "never had such a lovely girl rubbed his bottom before!" I must admit that is something I had never thought of doing! Also he discovered that this wonderful smiling girl was about on the verge of collapse, trying to do too much.

She and her husband lived in Croydon, from where she travelled to East Grimstead each day. Her husband was at college as a full-time student and she was still in part feeding and caring for her four month old baby girl. Each day she had to get up, feed and prepare her baby, take it to a neighbour, travel to the hospital, do a full day's work as a pupil nurse, training for her S.E.N. Then home again in the evening, often after 8.30 p.m., to fetch her baby, iron, cook and wash, and still have time to study for her final examinations in two months' time.

Matthew mentioned her to me and we introduced ourselves to each other. The following day, I talked to her and offered to have her baby stay with us completely until the end of March, when she took her final examinations. I took the precaution of writing down for her what we arranged, so that there should be no misunderstanding through failure of communication and language difficulty.

We arranged to have the babe as soon as our quarantine for measles expired, for £3 per week, until the end of March, and would treasure her for them. I felt that this was the right amount of money in their case, as her pay could not be too much, her husband was a student, and both were supported by the parents in Nigeria. They had been paying £2.50 a week to the neighbour for day care. She talked this over with her husband , and the following day said that they would like to do this.

I felt curiously cool now that the arrangement was made and we were to do something new for the first time in our lives. I did not know to what extent this was a loved and wanted child, and with full understanding of the dangers and the knowledge that anything in life can turn for good or bad, I just prayed the situation into God's hands, and asked that good might come out of it.

I had read Dr. John Bowley's "Child Care and the Growth of Love", written under the auspices of the World Health Organisation, and felt fully in agreement with his findings, so I knew the dangers to the baby and the family of taking the baby from the mother, but we felt this to be a critical situation. This could, we hoped, help

It was only afterwards that we were to learn of the Matron's and the Sister Tutor's worries for their nurse, who might soon collapse under the strain of doing too much, and would most certainly be unable to pass her examination. Later too we learned that only by living in at the hospital would she have completed enough hours practical work to take the examination, and hers was the only earned income.

2

Two weeks later, Bola arrived with a radiant Mummy and Daddy. Obviously a well-loved child, very well cared for, and full of sparkle and gurgles. Everything had come with her – cod liver oil, orange juice, powder, baby cream, everything in fact to make sure that she was the most beautiful baby in the world. The baby was in perfect condition, except for a large patch of cradle-cap scurf, and the parents were lovely. Augustine was twenty-six years old, thin, tall, and I think the most handsome man I had ever seen, and with a warm and gentle nature. Elizabeth, like many Nigerians, seemed to always be smiling, and appeared happy to entrust her precious baby to my arms. Bola was too young for us to explain what was happening – she was just four months old – so somehow we had to show her that all was well. I knew too that for this to be a successful venture, Elizabeth had to be, beyond doubt, happy about every detail, and I explained very warmly that I wanted them to visit and cuddle their baby just as much as was possible, so that the precious contact between herself and her baby was maintained. This baby must not be allowed to forget her parents, she must know beyond doubt that she belonged to them and was loved by them, in order that she should not get hurt too much.

Elizabeth and Augustine departed just before lunch, Matthew was back at business, Bola needed a feed, and Louise, seventeen months and Rosemary, just four, both seemed to need feeding or attention or something. Never have one pair of hands seemed so inadequate, Every time I put the baby down, she screamed and screamed, obviously aware that she was in stranger's house, but I had to make her feed. She was on one of the powdered milk feeds, and I had prepared everything I could for this moment, but oh dear, how very long boiled water or milk takes to cool when you are waiting! The baby was happy, no, quiet, so long as I cuddled her, and in our many happy hours together with Elizabeth and Augustine, I later learned that this is the Nigerian way – the baby is cuddled on the mother's back for the whole day, cradled safely in a special costume. So the English routine of keeping babies in a carry-cot all day with warm cuddles at feed and play times was quite foreign to her.

At this moment, the front door bell rang and there stood my first encounter with the officials that would ensure that all was correct and above board. I felt embarrassed, for it is one thing to be visited by the Child Care Officer when the situation is in hand, but to be caught with chaos reigning in the house and in one's heart…

I felt too that these officials are not exactly on one's side in the way that family doctors are a friend to the family, as a notice published in our local paper suggested, telling all prospective foster parents that failure to notify the Local Authority could mean a fine or imprisonment.

Any friend, however slight, would help, should they visit in a moment of crisis, whereas the Child Care Officer's job was to sit and talk to the mother of the family, and that this particular experience did not repeat itself – in all the visits so far, of about six different Local Authority Child Care Officers, not one had paid the normal good manner exchanges with our own children. I have the feeling that they may be satisfactory administrators, but that they in fact know very little about children.

We survived that first day and how deeply glad I was when Jackie came home from school, providing another pair of hands and arms to cuddle our little girlie.

Peter was terribly sweet, for with three sisters already, he could hardly condone us having another girl in the house. But we felt that as she was so young, we could take her into our hearts as a baby, not a little girl. I pointed out that in some language a baby is called "it", not he or she!

Gradually I was becoming more and more convinced that it was really boys we were short of in our family.

As the days went by, Bola settled in – she was not unhappy, but I knew she was a little too quiet and missed her Mummy. She lay a little too still as well and did not gurgle and chuckle for a few days and I longed to see her eyes sparkle again, as only those of a happy baby can. Each day her mummy phoned and after two days, she and Augustine came to see her, and give her those long hours of cuddle that she was used to. Interestingly, she did not recognise them this visit, but already looked to me for reassurance.

Peter was asking the most exciting questions at that time, questions which were really deep. He was six years old and these were his own thoughts entirely.

"Is the Bible true?

When was the Bible written?

Did Joseph put a seed in Mary to get Jesus?

Is Jesus God?

If Jesus is God, how can you kill God?

When a person is dead, can they come alive again?"

How difficult some were to answer truthfully!

Poor Bola! On one score I really felt for her! She had obviously been used to a quiet life, as indeed is any first child, and with all our squeals, shouts and bangs, she nearly jumped out of her skin. However, I knew that as long as she had long periods of quietness to rest properly, she would gradually become accustomed to the hurly-burly around her and then, of course, grow to positively enjoy it. Very soon she delighted in the company and antics of the children, who vied with each other to make her laugh.

The first three days passed quickly. I was tired out, having felt for this baby a certain emotional strain, but within a week, she was happier again, and I relaxed. Then on the following Monday, our storm broke.

3

It was Monday night, the day after Matthew started back to business after his convalescence. At one in the morning he awoke, writhing in terrible agony, and this continued without any relief throughout the whole night. The pain was in one loin and went on relentlessly and unbearably. At eight o'clock, I rang our Doctor, who normally took each Tuesday as his day off, and told him what was happening, for by now Matthew was more or less at the end of his tether, and asked that someone would call in and see him. He arrived an hour later and how very, very glad Matthew was to see him!

After a careful examination, he was unable to make a diagnosis at this early stage, but it looked like stones in the kidneys. He gave Matthew an injection of Pethedine with Pethedine tablets to take during the day, but Matthew's temperature was very high that night, and the Doctor came back again. It was fluids plus – plus – plus. I have never seen Matthew drink like this! I made sure that he drank one pint of warm liquid every two hours throughout the day from when he first woke up. Of course, all he did the whole time was to spend pennies, and all I seemed to do was give him drinks and empty his bottle. We had found an old vase which had the right accommodating shape, and this served admirably!

The second day a course of drugs was started, and still we searched for any bits of grit which Matthew might pass in his urine. This I did by pouring it into a clear glass bottle, but there was nothing to be seen, and he was still very ill.

That morning too, Jackie started to be ill, a bit languid, lying around when you would expect her to be playing, so she stayed at home from school. She slept on and off, and I fancied her eyes were just that tiny bit pink. And sure enough, three days later, this little miserable girlie got her measles spots.

And ten days later, and twelve days later, and thirteen days later, another miserable little girl, Rosemary, a fretful little Peter and a hollow-eyed little Louise all got their measles too. But still Bola stayed well, enjoying the twice weekly visits of her Mummy and Daddy.

The days went by and slowly everyone got better. Matthew was diagnosed as an acute epididymitis, which gradually responded to the drug, and the meals of homemade lemon barley began to be replaced by real food – surely a sign that he was getting better! The lemon barley was a great success, made in a huge four pint jug by squeezing the juice of lemons, adding brown sugar, and adding to this pints of water in which pearl barley had been boiled. The liquid was drained off, cooled, and added to the lemon and sugar and well stirred. It made such a smooth drink and I do not think he got too tired of it.

Then Bola seemed to get a little cold. She woke a lot at night, and on the third day her little spots arrived. "Well, what do little measles spots look like on a little brown tummy?" – everyone was curious to know. They come out as very dark brown spots instead of pink! But I was so very glad she only had it mildly.

Elizabeth was sweet, for she phoned that day and I told her that Bola had the measles, but was quite alright, not very ill and no need to worry. But within an hour she was here cuddling her little bundle and reassuring herself that all was well. No complications, just a straightforward measles, and she was soon over it and her normal healthy self again.

One curious thing which happened during this period was the visitors. Ever since Bola arrived, and throughout her stay, we had a constant stream of visitors, which was one aspect we had never considered. They fell roughly into four groups. The officials checking that we were behaving in a proper way; the folk who in genuine interest and affection for the Nigerians and Africans, came to see the baby and admire this beautiful child; the people who saw in us a facet to our nature that was new to them and came to see us; and the friends who came to visit our sick Daddy. And of course the Doctor and the parents. They were such delightful and much welcomed visitors. We enjoyed our visitors but I did, at times, find it tremendously tiring, for some days we had as many as seven visitors, in a continuous stream from nine in the morning until seven in the evening.

In the nine weeks that we had Bola, we had two visits from the

Child Care Officer, a pleasant man who had just joined the service. He seemed to feel that these must be yet one more pair of parents shelving their responsibility, not that they deeply loved this child and were, like so many desperately needing help, just to allow the mother to work well and earn for the family.

The Health Visitor made two calls and one more after Bola had gone, and one wondered what had been reported about a baby still in its nightdress and unbathed. How could the occasional visit possibly give the picture of over-all care, that T.L.C. (Tender Loving Care) that is all that matters to a child. (I had one official visitor every two weeks of Bola's stay)

What a lot of people who have been in Africa and perhaps Nigeria especially, have a real genuine love for these people and their babies. The babes seem even more beautiful than ours, perhaps because of their firm, big features. And several people said how very much they would have loved to adopt a coloured child, only their husbands would not bother. Rosemary was sweet one day when someone came up to admire the "black" baby. "She's not black," said Rosemary, "She's brown."

We had been very careful to tell the children the facts about colour without any prejudice. She had a brown silky skin because her Mummy and Daddy were Nigerian, and lived in the sunny part of the world. We had a fair skin because we were English and lived in the cooler part. And quite simply when a Nigerian marries an English girl, the child's skin comes out half way between.

I must admit to being quite terrified of Bola's hair when I first had her, for it seemed a mass of tight curls. But I talked to her mother about it and learned that it is more like a taut spring rather than a soft curl, and that it must just be washed normally and brushed thoroughly once each day. This is very painful to a young child, but has to be done, and, of course, looks and feels really beautiful when it is finished. So with a lot more confidence I undertook her hair-care, and soon, with a little olive oil, and a lot of time, cleared her head of the huge patch of cradle cap scurf. I also learned to brush gently!

What a crazy world this really is. Here are the English – God has given us straight hair – so we curl it. There are the Nigerians with heads of curly hair – so they straighten it. And here we are with our fair skins so we lie in the sun to try to get brown – unbelievable to the Africans who cherish the shade!

Quite a number of our visitors expressed how thrilled they were to see yet one more family who believed that integration of races was an absolute necessity for the future of the world. We had one call from a Doctor from South Africa who has already been in prison out there for his belief in equal opportunity and integration. How truly grateful they are that they have been able to come to Britain and find safety and sanctuary here.

Only once did we observe any prejudice against Bola because she was dark skinned, from neighbours, who tend to be very self assured in their own beliefs, and who seemed to have travelled about too little.

They were very happy days with Bola, and Augustine and Elizabeth. We saw a lot of them and encouraged them to stay here with their baby as long as possible each time, so that Bola should know her Mummy and Daddy. I knew that unless they were really encouraged to come, they would feel they were causing too much trouble in our busy household. So they came altogether twelve times in the nine weeks of Bola's stay, sometimes together and sometimes Elizabeth would come from the hospital with her friend. They would stay several hours, and cuddle their baby until she fell asleep in their arms.

Twice Bola went home to stay for a long weekend and came back so much happier, almost as though she was beginning to understand the situation, that she was deeply loved and belonged to them, and loved and welcomed by us.

It was very interesting for towards the end of her stay, several people hinted that the parents would just hive off and leave the baby. This I must confess gave me some days of panic. It just shows how dangerous gossip can be, For none of these people, except the Child Care Officer had any real experience of these things, and it was not in keeping of what I knew of the parents. We had grown to love Augustine and Elizabeth, and all our children longed for their visits, but I had to admit what I did not want to admit. I was growing increasingly tired, and a mother cannot afford to be too tired with young children at home, for she must be able to go on all day, and all night as well when some little person is fretful, or cold or hungry, or teething or something else makes them miserable in the night. And how very tired one can be. I think it is the perpetual responsibility, as well as the plain hard work, for only if someone else is watching over one's cherubs can one allow oneself to go off into a really deep sleep. How often one's sleep is just very light, so that the very second that one hears the baby cough in the night, one is out of bed in a flash to check that it is not choking. As with my own babies, I always slept with Bola only a few feet away from me so that I should hear if anything was amiss with her.

With the £3 that I received from Elizabeth and Augustine each week, I paid a dear friend, a clergyman's wife 4/- an hour to come for 2 ½ hours each week to look after the children and let me go out on my own (10/-). Then Bola had about 11 ½ pints of milk each week at 10 ½ d. per pint, approximately 10/-, washing powder for the extra washing 4/-, three eggs 1/-. This came to 25/- leaving me a mighty bonus of 35/- per week for 165 ½ hours, out of which I still had to buy baby shampoo, Milton, teats, plastic pants and zinc and castor oil cream, rose hip syrup. All her small quantities of food were out of our normal family diet. Clearly at a rate of around 2 ½ d. an hour I was not going to make a fortune!

Obviously too I needed some help in the house. I could see that I was losing ground slowly with the housework, for I was tired, and though Matthew is a jolly good husband, he is a very normal man, which means that his capacity for looking after children and doing housework, in addition to his own busy job, is strictly limited!

So, with a further two visits to the Doctor to get her vaccination to take, we carefully packed up all Bola's things, and, as originally arranged, at the end of March Augustine and Elizabeth took Bola home.

Elizabeth had taken her examination and how very much we hoped she would pass. Augustine was now at home on college vacation and could look after his small daughter, who already so obviously delighted in her daddy, until Elizabeth could get a part-time nurses job after the results came through.

We had loved having Bola, and were grateful for all the interest she had brought into our life, but truly I was too tired now, and I was glad she had gone. But I hoped that we had all learned something. Bola – that there are warm, kind people around, albeit harassed, when things seem wrong. Elizabeth and Augustine – to take heart when they feel hurt by any prejudice they meet in England. Matthew and I – that two people trusted us with their most precious treasure, and our children – I think they will grow up loving Nigerians for a very long time.

4

I learnt a number of things having Bola. Fostering is so important in our England today, where for one reason or another, more and more children are in care, or in a private foster home, and it is time that an attempt was made to educate foster mothers in their work and recompense them in a more realistic way. There is a big difference between being a good mother and being a good foster parent. For in any case where a child is in care and has a loving mother of any sort, working, unsupported, ill or homeless, it is imperative that the very utmost contact is maintained with the real mother, and both parents, if this is possible. This contact must be as often as possible in the natural setting of the foster home. This will demand a mature and generous outlook on the part of the foster parent, for only a really warm and generous hostess is going to make the real mother want to come as often as she can and be with her child,

I think too that the children must be accredited with a sense of knowing the truth, and only being told the truth all the time will help them to live with their own very considerable difficulties. Perhaps it would be better to call foster mothers foster Aunties in England now, where even a remote mother exists, in order that every possible chance is given for the child to avoid confusion and so understand from very early days that they have a mummy, who is unable to look after them, so Auntie does instead. This is normal language the child's world understands and a situation understood by all children, and one which has status in their world.

It also brought home to me the great need for many day nurseries, all easily accessible, so that the many people forced to make, very often much less accessible private arrangements in fosterings, could place their children in a day nursery and still collect them at night. To work well though, these day nurseries would have to be open for much longer hours than just 8.30 until 5.00 p.m. to allow the mothers to do a greater variety of work. I do not think it is realised just how very many unsupported mothers, wives of students, or wives of very low-paid workers, simply must work to earn money, and this cannot be done satisfactorily without adequate care of the children. The children would achieve a better level of mental health with this arrangement than the awful isolation that they may suffer when away from the parent in a nursery or foster home.

This reminds me of a real-life situation. I heard about an unsupported mother who'd had a nervous breakdown and was admitted to hospital. Her two sons, lovely boys of eight and ten, were committed into care on a court order, and separated into two *different* local authority Children's Homes, and as a result, two different schools. On asking to see their mother, they were refused.

This seems so wrong on every account, for the children are essential to help in the mother's recovery. They too must be allowed to grow strong together so that in only a very few years they will all be able to help each other, and the boys support the mother. Perhaps in our over sentimental attitude to protect the children, we are in danger of failing to realise that a child needs its mother more than anyone else, however inadequate, apparently, she may be, by our standards. Very often, real and loving help of a very practical nature would be of the greatest long term help for everyone. For today's is but tomorrow's adult, and the hurt we do to the child today in taking him away from his mother may go with him, leaving a bitter scar right into adulthood. Somehow in order to help a child grow to maturity, we must help them face and overcome their difficulties, not remove them from those difficulties.

One last point which came to my notice when Bola was with us was about the availability of foster parents. It is problematical that for private fosterings the Local Authority has to go through the whole childcare routine for all the children placed for longer than a month. This has two adverse effects. One is that a number of people who love children and would do this sort of work are not willing to put up with yet one more encroachment of personal liberty, and be registered and inspected, and subjected to the scrutinising eye of the Authorities.

A friend of Elizabeth's also working at the local hospital, had her husband at Bristol University, and her fifteen month old baby boy in London where he has been with a lovely foster family since a few months old. The mother was only able to get in to see him about once a month, and in spite of everything she could do, the child rejected her as his mother, and quite naturally, chose the foster parents. This was a tricky situation, which perhaps could be improved by finding a foster home very near the hospital, where the mother, who loved this child, could visit him often and take him out and re-establish herself, to start with as a constant visitor and dear friend to the child. I found a family on the council estate who would take the child (their daughter's child had just gone and left a gap in their lives), but on being told that she would have to register and be inspected and visited, they turned it down.

The other effect of this all is to dry up the supply of desperately needed holiday homes for those children with mothers who must work, and somehow manage in term time, but for whom the school holidays are a veritable nightmare. So often boarding school holidays are longer than the statutory month allowed for a child to be a paying guest without registering.

5

In due course we heard from Elizabeth to say that she had passed her examination. Well done, Elizabeth! She told us that it took Bola two and a half days to accept Elizabeth as her mother on taking her home and this in spite of us maintaining such a good contact between them. At the time of going home, she was 6½ months old.

We did not see them for a few months and then as the time came for Bola's first birthday, Elizabeth rang and invited all the children to her party. The children were thrilled, and were bathed, and dressed in their best clothes, until they looked a really gorgeous bunch of poppets, each carrying a tiny gift for little Bola. Augustine insisted on fetching them all in his car, and what a treat it was for us to be on our own for a couple of hours. The children all came back absolutely radiant and Augustine absolutely exhausted! He had carried Louise around continuously, at her special request. What a wonderful party it must have been with a lot of Nigerian children and a lot of little English children, all sharing Bola's day together.

The Nursery

1

Ever since we moved into the delightful part of the country, just over a year ago, I have made such an interesting study for myself. I felt that any child that we took into our family must, for one reason or another, be a "sticker", one that was without any family contact and would need a permanent home. These children I knew existed but it is difficult to find them. They are a very small proportion of the children in care, but I knew that there must be some somewhere. So I searched in magazines and newspapers for advertisements put into the personal columns. During the year, I found about eight children, through my first enquiry by letter, who would be available for adoption. These I followed up after an interval of about three months, and in every case the child had been found a family where it would go for fostering with a view to adoption. Certainly, in our lovely England, there was a wealth of goodwill and warmth of nature abounding. If only people knew of the need, there would be help.

Just near our home was a nursery run by a voluntary society, and so I went there to visit and look for myself. The Matron was charming and allowed me to look around and talk to the children. I had previously asked our Area Children's Officer if I could visit our Local Authority Nursery, for which permission was refused. The visit was followed by more visits when I took our children in turns, and we stayed, often for a long time, playing and talking to the children and the nursery nurses. They were delightful girls who handled the children warmly and intelligently.

My first visit followed very closely on the reading of Dr. John Bowlby's book, and I was interested to see exactly what he talks about, but so very subtle that it would be easy to miss. This was a very happy, contented nursery, there was no doubt about that, with a very high staffing/baby ratio – with one nurse to every babe, and each babe had his own special nurse. Though, with some of the staff on holiday, some on nights, off sick and days off, and others at college during their course, it worked out in practice about two nurses to each group of seven children. What fantastic devotion to duty this grand Matron had, for with only one other Staff member over twenty one years old, she always had to be there when that Sister was off.

I was so happy to be there, for it is often a long and boring day for children, as all we mothers know, and once, when there was a staff crisis and I had gone on my own, I was asked if I would help with bathing the "blue room". They were the babies between about ten months and eighteen months. Each had to be bathed, seven altogether, and one nurse and I had about an hour to spend over the children. It was fun and I found it so interesting. Only one of the babes resented me doing them, although I did not know these children and was really a stranger to them. The others were passively warm, showing neither hostility not enthusiasm about a stranger attending to them. I felt that most children in normal families at this age would not take kindly to a stranger, doing this most intimate thing of bathing them.

I had always felt myself able to make contact with a child if I tried, but I could not get the children to play in the water or respond to the usual baby bathtime games like ride-a-cock-horse and this-little-piggy-went-to-market. They just sat quite happy, passively, hardly aware, it seemed that they'd had their bath – a very special time of play and contact. The nurses at this nursery tried very hard too to play all the lovely baby games, and do all the normal mother things, but I felt that the response was without enthusiasm and the pleasure that a normal baby gets. One baby hated my intrusion and protested violently to being messed about by a stranger not wearing an overall, and this I felt was more normal.

Over these months, I had watched the progress with interest of one little babe, a fat little bundle called Nicola. She was seven months when I met her first and then she seemed very normal to me. I loved cuddling this child and, on finding that she was for adoption, wrote to the Child Care Officer concerned, in a general way, asking about their children, wondering in my heart if we could have this wee girlie. After a very long time, a reply visit came, and how we enjoyed it, a Child Care Officer who seemed to talk our sort of language!

But several points were made plain. Under no circumstances could we choose a child, we would not be considered for a child until Louise, our youngest, was over two years old and never was it possible to place a child "into" the family. That meant that an adopted child could not be placed in among our natural children, but only in a natural position after our own babies had finished. And clearly printed on that very first form was the statement that only people unable to have their own children would be considered for adoption.

It seemed that I was batting on the wrong wicket. I was young (34 exactly!) very fertile, and now intended not to have any more of my own children. I have complete faith in family planning methods – so long as they are used – and used properly! But one thing was certain. For me, and no doubt others too, it would not matter if the family planning contraceptives failed, or we decided in the far future to have another baby. We could love all our children, adopted or natural.

2

I talked a lot to the nurses at the nursery and to Matron, and gradually discovered the children who were for adoption. Beautiful, fine, healthy children whose only real need was a mummy and daddy who was really theirs, their heritage. It seemed that if a baby was not adopted very early on, its chances of achieving adoption lessened with every month that went by. There was Jeremy, a gentle boy of three and a quarter, a handsome child with dark hair, brown eyes and a slightly dusky skin, of Anglo-West Indian parents. Anita was a marvellous child, tall, independent, and mature for her two and a half years and completely English. She had a hare lip which had been very skilfully repaired and she was just left with a narrow pink scar and no disability from it. She talked well and so obviously needed a Mummy. She alone called me Mummy and asked me to do those little special things that only Mummies do so often. She'd had a fantastic experience, for adoptive parents were found for this little girlie and after the usual and careful long introductions she went to join her new Mummy and Daddy, to be sent back a short while later at the age of two, because she was too strong willed.

How very sad, for parents with experience of children know that some children are like this, and can only be firmly loved into a happy state of reasonableness. Perhaps families with children should be encouraged to take the older children, for with experience one gradually comes not to be surprised at anything!

Pippa was a quiet little girlie of two, very sweet, and English. Then little Nicola. She had grown into a beautiful babe of one year old, just starting to walk, with dark brown hair full of gentle curls, brown eyes and a hint of summer brown in her skin. She was of Anglo-Indian parents. Stuart was a handsome, English babe of about fifteen months, needing a little more plastic surgery to his penis, but with a promise by the surgeons that they would make him perfect. There was however a slight doubt that he would be quite perfect, but surely somewhere in our country there was a family who could love this boy all his life and help him grow into a strong and happy person, able to accept the fact that even if he were not to be a father, he and his wife could fill their home with their own adopted children.

Sarah was about one year old – a child full of smiles and making normal progress in every way. But her background was bad, and normally prospective adopters are told the history before seeing the child – so she never got as far as being seen by parents wanting a child.

Once again, I wrote to their Child Care Officer explaining that we wanted to take an older child, a boy of five years old to fit between Peter and Rosemary, into our home for life, and would they please consider us. After nearly two months, a telephone call came in reply, offering me no hope whatever. I was furious and lost my temper, and very firmly mentioned that I even knew that there was one little boy named Jeremy in our local nursery who needed a Mummy and Daddy. For the first time, she showed interest in our idea.

3

After a very short interval, I wrote to her asking specifically if we could have Jeremy. Again the reply came that there was very little hope, as it had become general policy not to place children in between natural children in a family. Again we wrote and persuaded her to visit us and get to know us better. This she did twice, and we found her charming and delightful with the children. At the same time, she was able to get a glimpse of us as a family, and bless her, she decided, unknown to us, to plead our cause with London.

It was interesting how I found that in my searches I had now gone right round in a full circle. It seemed that we could not be happy as foster parents to a child, when so often it seemed that it was the whole family that needed the help. How could I care for a baby of an unmarried mother, when I desperately believed that they should be cared for and helped together? How could I look after a child made homeless when I felt that taking children away from their parents, at this time of crisis, was a positively bad and most damaging thing? At no time did I want to be a party in the very things I disagreed with.

Gradually, I came to see that for us it would need to be adoption, for only in this way could we commit ourselves with total love to a child whose own family ties had been broken. How could I face a child in his questioning teens with the thought "Mummy, if you say you love me, why did you not adopt me?" So my cherished dream of having children in the family and having the financial burden taken from me would have to go, and we would have to trust that there would be enough money, and resort to other ways of my supplementing Matthew's excellent, just adequate, income.

We filled in the adoption form, and the Child Care Officer pleaded our cause, and so did the nursery Matron where Jeremy was living, also without my knowledge.

It seemed that the reluctance to allow a child to be placed in between natural children was due to the very high breakdown rate of children fostered out in this situation. We could have a young baby, but that was not what we wanted.

So I wrote the following letter to London – our very last hope to get Jeremy into our family:

> *Dear Sir,*
> *In my search for a child to come into our family, I have three criteria: (i) That the child's attachment to the natural parents should be irrevocably broken; (ii) That in taking a child, I should not merely deprive another mother of a child for which she longed; (iii) That the child should fit into a natural gap in our family.*
>
> *Now we have found Jeremy, a little boy of three and a half years old, at – Nursery, and both Matthew and I know that we can give this child a warm welcome, and the sort of enduring love that would help him to grow into a happy and mature person.*

Jeremy fulfils all the criteria and we long that you will allow Jeremy to come into our family to be our true son.

I know that we can make a success of this venture, and we would see him, and all our children, through all the behaviour problems, and personal difficulties, as and when they arise.

Jeremy is three years younger than Peter, our other son. This would give them the chance to relate together as brothers, and be good companions. I consider that this "gap" is the widest to allow much relationship to develop between two children.

I want an integrated family (this seems even more important with mixed race children) so that the casual outsider does not know at a glance which are the natural and which are adopted children.

We are hoping to move to a larger house soon with plenty of accommodation and space for us all to grow as individuals.

Naturally, before asking for this child, a lot of careful preparation has been done in our family, so that we are all emotionally ready to bring Jeremy into our home and hearts. (Even his Teddy is waiting for him)

The chances of his growing to full mental and emotional maturity in adulthood are certainly more if he is not forever deprived of the disciplines and love, the troubles and laughter, that are the constant pattern of a normal family life.

We can, with your support, be one of the successful 10% of in-placements. Surely, it is worthwhile.

Yours very sincerely,
(signed) Diana Macdonald

This letter was followed up with an appointment to see the great man himself, the Head of the boarding-out department, whose decision it was ultimately to say yes or no to each adoption request. How we longed for him to say yes, though Matthew said he never doubted that when he had seen us and talked with us, he would do so.

I knew that there would be behaviour disturbances in the children, for any new situation produces its own strains, but I felt that we could handle these and live through them. Of course, I had cold feet at times, but then doing any new big thing would make one feel nervous. I remember how I felt when I took off my L-plates, after passing my driving test, to be told that I could now drive, alone, for the very first time, right out of the centre of Nottingham.

Of course, we had been taking considerable trouble to prepare the children for what we were doing and, as is our policy, kept them completely informed about the situation. A part of this was the buying of Jeremy's teddy. All our children had had a teddy from Matthew and me for their first birthday, so we bought Jeremy's teddy. It was the very nicest teddy, for each time we had bought the loveliest teddy the shop had to offer, and it was one that everyone would be pleased to play with – a very necessary bargaining power.

So the day came for our interview. All the children were put out with friends, Rosemary and Louise all day, and Jackie and Peter after school. We were off to London. What a real treat it was to out on our own. I wondered why we needed such an excuse as this – surely we could go just for nothing, one day!

4

The interview went well. Matthew assured me that he would do the interviewing and that dispelled my interview nerves to a certain extent. The buildings in which the administration was done were deplorable, and it seemed a miracle that so many human lives were helped in such surroundings.

After long talks lasting an hour and a quarter, the interview was over. We had found Mr. X utterly charming, and clearly concerned with the welfare of the children in their care. Very knowledgeable too, on all the subjects surrounding children deprived of a normal family life. To our question, at the very end of the interview, he said that we could have Jeremy.

I felt curiously cool, and Matthew said he knew that would be the answer. I wondered, now that there was some actual news to tell the children, how they would take it. In particular, I felt in a panic about Peter's reaction, as all along he had maintained that it had to be a boy nearer his age, about five and a half.

But I need not have worried, for as soon as we picked him up he asked, "Did you get Jeremy?"

"Yes," I replied.

"Good." And that was the end of that.

We'd had a lovely day. While waiting for the time to pass before the interview, we had a scrumptious Chinese luncheon at The Lotus House and wandered for the first time down the famous Kings Road, Chelsea. This was sheer luxury to me, and the sun was streaming down, making all the gay mini-dresses look so dinky. In one of those junky-antique shops, we spotted a round mahogany table which Matthew and I both felt would look super in our lounge. So in a very gay mood we bought it. Oh, what a treat to buy something beautiful and solid as a souvenir of that day!

5

Now I felt that I had always had Jeremy as one of my children, and that he was away from home in the nursery, rather as I imagined mothers feel who have to leave their children in hospital. I now worried about him, as when our children were staying away for the night, and wished that I could care for him without further delay.

We now had to wait for a further visit by the Child Care Officer, who had to see us both together, then each of us had to have a medical, the Vicar had to be interviewed, and also our referee in Birmingham.

The doctor was very amusing during my medical.

"Have you anything that you know will shorten your life?"

"Yes, children."

"No," he replied softly, "children don't kill you, they drive you barmy!" He had four himself!

With all the forms completed by everybody, our application had to be passed formally by a Committee, and then a letter would come to say that we could start bringing Jeremy home and taking him out on our own.

The weeks went by, weeks during which my delight in the whole business turned to irritation, and then even that started to wear off. I started to forget about Jeremy. I was, in fact, winding down emotionally. This alarmed me very much. The wait had gone on too long for me. It was now four and a half months since our first momentous decision when we wrote and asked for an older child. Two and a half months since I had asked specifically for Jeremy and six weeks since they had said yes in London. Not long really, but too long for me. I badly needed to get started.

So I made another telephone call to try to hurry things up and, at the same time, I took some of the nursery children home several times, always including Jeremy. This helped a bit, but I could not help feeling that precious time in his early childhood was simply being wasted. "Children are homemade and outward bound", I had heard somewhere and this was certainly how I felt.

Every time I went to the nursery, I felt filled with gloom, for in my eyes, the environment seemed like a prison, when compared with the normal freedom of a family. Sometimes I cried inside when I saw the hopelessness of those special children who were placed for adoption as babies, and who didn't get a family. Surely I felt that if only people knew about these children, they would go. Fancy arriving at an age of understanding, and knowing that you had been placed for sale, as it were, and no one wanted you, even though you were, in fact, being given away.

Children's eyes shine. These children's eyes did not shine, though they were not unhappy. But though they were given every single care, and they were cared for superbly and loved in a general way, because they did not have the one thing they really needed, a family of their own, all the other care, as it were, counted for nothing. Still they were dying inside themselves.

Two more children were then added to the nursery – two adoption breakdowns. These two girlies had both been out for a year or so with their adopted parents and it had not worked out. This is one of the beastly unavoidable tragedies of life, where closely related personalities are just not compatible. In human relationships, it just is not possible to know what makes two people be happy together, and a child who has been in a nursery and short of mother love is going to be a long time before he is able to accept love from new parents and give it back, sometimes a very long time. Miranda was a wee girl of three and a half, of Anglo-West Indian parents, who weighed less than when she went out a year ago. Shirley was three and a half, an enchanting all English child. The relationship with the adopting family had never matured and she was now wet and soiling both day and night. A most beautiful child, full of charm and intelligence.

It is not all sad stories though, for so many of these nursery children are deeply loved by one parent and go back to them just as soon as they can manage to look after them.

6

Several days after my telephone call to our delightful and sensitive Child Care Officer, she sent word that we could take Jeremy out alone and so we brought him home for a couple of short visits. It was pleasant but a little too high-powered to last, as each one of us consciously wanted to give him a great deal of our abounding attention.

On July 28th we had word, by letter, that we had been accepted as prospective adopters for Jeremy and that arrangements would be made to move him to our home on the "boarding-out-with-a-view-to-adoption" scheme. We knew that he had to be introduced into our family gradually to help the adjustment of both Jeremy and our children, so for the first time he came for one night only. Then later for two nights. The second time was definitely easier than the first, but I was emotionally exhausted. It was after this second visit that I was completely overtaken by panic – I do not think that I have ever been so panic-stricken before. To a certain extent, it was the knowledge that if I failed, someone was going to get very, very hurt. I also did not know how I would react to the additional strains, imposed on us all. I realised now that I had waited too long, and thought too much about the whole subject.

This panic amounted to terror – but I felt that probably every major new venture is preceded by this sort of feeling, for one has no previous related experience to call on. I had just read a book which helped me through those few days. "With love to the Church", by Monica Furlong. The writer, a Christian, had said that perhaps the most difficult thing for a Christian to do was to look clearly at herself, and then seeing herself, to go forward with Jesus.

This was what I did. In prayer I lifted my utter panic into God's presence, and then slowly, one by one, put myself, then Matthew, then Jackie, then Peter, then Rosemary, then Louise, then Jeremy, then all of us together into the presence of Christ in my imagination. This is how I normally pray and, from practice, I know that prayer works, not asking prayers, but simply committing ourselves to Christ and then He can do what He wants for the best.

Jeremy

1

And so on 10th August, exactly three months after I asked for him, and at the beginning of the school holidays, just Jackie, Rosemary and I went to fetch Jeremy. He was waiting so eagerly, a little boy of three years and eight months. As always, smiling, he had been well prepared by the nursery for the move. Touchingly, his clothes and his own special toys were all in a paper bag, his clothes so clearly cared for, and the child looking radiant. His nursery nurse had already brought some of his toys to our house, and at the same time, we inherited Twiggles, a guinea pig, Jeremy's guinea pig. Oh dear, I felt I had enough troubles without another guinea pig!

With Jeremy came his own little prayers and photograph album, a milk token, a letter to the Ministry of Social Security for another milk token book, a Health Service card, and a record of all his illnesses, immunisations and vaccinations. I was allowed to keep a carefully compiled adoption medical, which stated what I could see for myself – that Jeremy was physically and mentally normal. It told me too about his natural parents, and gave me a case history of how the whole situation had come about. Like most children placed for adoption in this country both his parents were still living. His father was a high class Indian, a Brahmin. I did not know what this meant and was curious to know! He was a student and his mother also a young commerce student at the time of Jeremy's birth.

Certainly, from what I had seen of this wee boy he had a normal, good intelligence. He had dark hair; lovely shiny almost black hair, dark brown eyes, and what I would describe as a lightly tanned skin. His nails were slightly bitten, he wet the bed still at night, and was purported to get septic very easily! But as far as I was concerned, he was in a perfect condition with just a catarrhy nose.

He had a wonderful sense of fun and was very much "All Boy"! On the two visits to us, he had already gone through two pairs of trousers – and how I hate mending! After his first bath, when he must have drunk at least a pint of bath water while playing with the tooth mugs, he was soaked through in the night, and so here was something I decided would have to go! Now our bath is filled only with toys that cannot be drunk out of, and I guard the tooth mugs zealously. And by potting him two hours after going to bed and then again when we go to bed, and limiting his evening drink to one cup of milk at 4.0 p.m. we made progress at night.

He was already "into things" and twice I found him dangling from our old farm cart in the garden – once by his sleeve, and once he had slipped through a hole in the floor of the cart, to wait there, just his legs visible, and trapped until someone rescued him. He was quite drunk with the freedom that was now his and was enjoying it all so much.

Twiggles proved to be a great success and one morning, we put him under a laundry basket with a brick on top while we cleaned out his cage. When everyone had forgotten about him, the laundry basket started to glide all over the lawn. Twiggles's snout was firmly stuck through the side of the basket, and he was off! Never before had we seen an upside-down laundry basket move so fast!

The subject of Jeremy's arrival puzzled one little girl visitor, and so I used the opportunity to go through with Jeremy how his adoption had arisen. We had already told our children this several times as factually as possible, and this was the story I shall stick to with Jeremy. His Mummy and Daddy loved each other but they were not able to get married. When he was born, his Mummy loved him very much but because she was not married she could not look after him, and so she asked the nursery to look after him, and so she asked the nursery to look after him and find another family to adopt him.

I think it important for them to know that they were conceived in love, and that they were loved by their mothers. As we do not know for certain that it was any way but this, the situation ought to be given the benefit of the doubt.

2

I was still nervous at the prospect of telling my family who, unused to large families, felt that four was already far too many. Oh dear, how could I tell them we were now five? I felt Amimbola might have paved the way for us. I never could send the letter I had prepared for them, for this was how I really wanted to write to everyone to share our news:

> *My dears,*
> *Once again we have some lovely news for you. The taking of a child into a family. There has been a very long search, a long period of waiting, careful preparations, and the expectant thrill of getting things ready. Then the tremendous upheaval of all our lives, and the feeling of pride and contentment , as one more little person with a new Mummy and Daddy settles into the new routine.*
>
> *Very soon, we too are expecting this happy event, as Jeremy, a little boy of three comes into our family – waiting – now unknowing – to begin a new life. To be re-born. For his whole life he has been in a nursery , never knowing the love of a Mummy and Daddy and family around him.*
>
> *Now he will learn, as so many others have, the meaning of living, learn to laugh easily and naturally, to feel safe*

and unafraid. Learn, above all what it is to be loved, with understanding and firmness, with cuddles and bedtime kisses, tussles with Daddy, and family picnics. And learn, in time, to love back.

With our warmest love to you both,
God Bless,

However, trying to be fair to all of us and to our parents, I sent a brief note to them both, with a very cheerful photograph of Jeremy, taken before he came to us. The reaction was very much as I expected, but none the less agonising. A torrent of abuse came from my mother, who I knew would feel desperate about the situation. She was frankly furious, and assured me that she would never get over such a thing. It was unthinkable that, with four very beautiful children, we should not be content; and think, in years to come, when our dear adopted boy would cause endless trouble in the family. She knew of a family who had taken a child, and the result was chaos and misery for everyone. Without doubt, the real sin was that we should have a half-caste in the family – this she repeated endlessly in letters and telephone calls. Thankfully my parents lived one hundred and fifty miles away, and could not easily call on us, otherwise I do not honestly think that at that stage I would have been strong enough to bear this pain. I was terribly upset, but none of the children knew about the situation. If it had continued, it would have meant that we would see even less of my Mother and Father.

My Father was upset from a different point of view, and wrote tender and loving letters, in which he discussed my personal deprivation, and questioned a lot about money. How were we going to manage, and afford to educate our family? I did not know the answers. But I also felt that it is more important than ever that some of the coloured children have a very good education, and achieve the maximum of which they are capable.

The onslaught from my parents went on, but we hoped that when they saw us all happily together and me, I hoped not looking like a down-trodden Mum, perhaps they would not feel so upset. Matthew's Father was delighted and accepted it as the most natural thing in the world. But I felt that at that stage I could stand no more abuse and so did not tell him that Jeremy was a bit of a mixture. No doubt he would hear via the grape vine soon enough!

In a lot of older people's eyes, we were doing something very terrible. "They should go back where they belong" was a feeling that was voiced, but, of course, "they" do not belong anywhere. It was strange to find that friends were not necessarily well-wishers. But how I gathered strength when someone gave me a word of encouragement. People said, so well meaningly, such terrible things, but I had thought through most of them before Jeremy arrived, and how very grateful we were when we encountered genuine sympathy. It was still very early days.

We were so very glad, for among our friends is a Surgeon from our local hospital, an Indian over here to study plastic surgery, and our friendship with him has given us another natural opportunity to discuss skin colour and mixed marriages with the children, and clearly to them it is completely straight forward, with no complications – rather like mixing paints in a paint box. There were no prejudices and no problems to them.

I had fully expected to send out little notelets to announce Jeremy's arrival, with letters only to very dear friends, but I found that I was too tired, and too emotionally involved to cope with everyone's varied and unexpected reactions. So I left it for our friends to find out in a natural way. I could not be sure of a single person's reaction, but I felt that probably people would feel very different if they met Jeremy and his appealing ways, rather than being confronted with a theory which often went against the grain.

But we were happy, and I think more at peace as a family.

3

We all settled down marvellously after we fetched Jeremy from the nursery.

He had come willingly into my arms, and was clearly glad at last to have a Mummy and a Daddy. I was so very glad that he had been told the truth at the nursery and I would do the same, so that we would not start on that awful path of living a lie, if we could avoid it.

The first few days I was tired out, as I felt anxious that they should pass rather smoothly, and how very glad I was to sit down late the first night with the very largest glass of wine – what a warm relaxer!

He seemed happy and at peace. He had a medical the day before coming to us, and was pronounced perfect, but in fact his nose was full of infection, not a cold, but continually wet and sneezing out large amounts of infected mucous. His legs were not straight, with about one and a quarter inches of knock knee, which could not be corrected. He was still wetting at night, and his little nails were bitten. His back was very rounded and his little body was not as flexible as I felt it should be for his age. But he was cheerful and talked endlessly in a high pitched screech.

There were many things which we took for granted that he had never experienced in life. All the time we kept encountering those things which our children had grown up with naturally. One thing which clearly shattered him was the sight of naked adult bodies. To us it seems perfectly natural that in a family we should sometimes be naked, but the size of everything shattered him! Daddy's nakedness must have seemed very big compared to the tiny bodies of the children he had seen in the nursery!

Very soon we realised that he could not run properly. Although they were well-endowed with space at the nursery, every space was safely confined with a fence around, so that never had he run in an open space. He tended to just scuttle away from people to hide his shyness. He was also terrified of heights and was panic stricken when the children suggested that they all take turns jumping from the old dining room table.

I was very self-conscious about the increase in my family but I realised that the novelty would soon wear off, and folk would accept and forget the situation. I decided that I would not force my own emotions, but, as with a new baby, let them develop naturally. I realised that with all the other children, the situation was a complicated one, but how thrilled I was at the end of one week to hear myself say, "I love you, darling" as I tucked him up at night.

We talked quite a lot about the nursery when we were alone, as he missed the other nursery children who were his very dear friends. Every time we went into town, he asked to go back to the nursery, but I felt that if ever we went back there, it must be after a long period with us, and after he felt he belonged to our family. No doubt the sheltered environment of a nursery, orphanage or prison where all responsibility is taken away from the individual, are so much easier and less painful, than the hard, tough, cruel jungle of the real world outside. It is, of course, this that makes the adjustment to normal life so difficult.

His lack of a single mother figure attachment did not show itself until very markedly, as he had a warm nature, and has, thankfully, received a lot of warm, generous and loving handling at the nursery.

Clearly he had received tender loving care, for his clothes and toys were lovingly and sensitively cared for. But his eyes were a bit flat and did not shine as those of well-loved children in families. One day in a park, he went up to another woman and put his arm around her – a complete stranger. In other words, all grown-ups were equally his friends. I had to establish myself as someone different, and more special than all other grown-ups to him, so that later he could love just the one woman whom he would marry. For I felt that it was from one single loving and satisfactory relationship with his wife.

We spoke about babies – where did babies come from. Oh,

Jeremy, when first he came to us

certainly, that was something he did know – "from the nursery." It was going to be difficult for him to understand that babies come out of mummies tummies, until he could experience it in someone whom he knew. This experience I did not intend to provide!

We had just been to see the film "Born Free" and it seemed as though it had a special significance for me. Were we in time I wondered, and was I skilful enough, and would circumstances permit us to allow Jeremy's emotions to develop normally, or would this long period of deprivation and the forever knowledge that his Mummy and Daddy had not kept him but placed him for adoption, prevent him from coming to terms with his own emotions and allow him to learn to love, deeply.

Jeremy had a glorious sense of fun and loved nothing more than to be slightly mischievous. One day on a building site, he found a 'loo' in the garden, waiting to be plumbed into the house. With an obvious glint in his eye and the certain knowledge that he was being an imp, he used the toilet to "spend a penny"!

It was a very busy period. There were some major complications for me, and of course my domestic help who came one afternoon a week was ill and so the house got grubbier and grubbier. Jeremy descended on us at the beginning of nine weeks of summer school holiday – not what one's high-powered organisation would choose! Louise slept on a camp bed, and somehow we managed – with a very great deal of mess in one very small house.

But the children gave me strength – in turn providing some spark of humour or kindness. One day Rosemary came home with two little children from the village – "Mummy, can they have a little turn in our family now?" I knew just what she meant, I felt sure.

4

Within a few days of his coming, it was clear that Jeremy was beginning to be ill, and it was on the third day that he began to cough endlessly and wheeze loudly. By the night, he was very ill, and tossed the whole time wailing, coughing, sweating a cold clammy sweat, and wheezing continuously. We called the doctor in the morning and he came often that day, for I was at a disadvantage in not really knowing the child. To start with, we did not know what was wrong with Jeremy, but as the treatment was successful, it turned out to be an acute attack of bronchitis. This was all quite new to me, as never before had I seen a case, and how very ill he was. Of course I wondered if he had pneumonia, or had inhaled a little piece of plastic, with some lung collapse, but an X ray ruled out those two possibilities. In the early days, we all wondered if at least in part it was the psychological reaction to being faced with the big wide world, but the doctor was willing to go along with me – we had to rule out every possible physical cause before deciding that this illness was entirely psychological, for to start with it looked so like asthma. The doctor, and everyone were very kind, for it was decided that if Jeremy needed intensive care, or hospital care that I could not provide, Matron would have him back at the nursery.

Fortunately, none of this was necessary, and he recovered quickly and uneventfully, but he was still left with a very bad cough, several times in the day and night, which left him breathless and gasping, and a dripping sinus, which I still felt was the cause of all the trouble. I felt that we could, in time, get these cleared up.

Then, to crown it all, he developed septic spots all over his head which took a long time to clear up. It took many visits to Doctors before we realised that they were just septic insect bites. Our family was not normally bitten, and I suppose everyone who is bitten knows how to deal with them, so it was the last thing we all thought of!

He was so deprived really, his deprivation being that of a child brought up in an institution, for whom no substitute mother had been provided. So many little things we encountered each day were unnatural. It took so long for him to realise that I actually had to make the cake – it did not just fall from the skies. He put his hand right into the gas flame – I think he had never seen one before. The bath defeated him if it were a trace too hot or too cold, and he would scream hysterically, "It's burning me." He had no experience to tell him simply to add a little cold water! It was never, of course, hot enough to burn him, but no doubt was not that same even temperature that the trained nursery nurses would use for the babies' baths. He was in fact very short of home-made experience.

A whole apple was quite beyond him. He ate incessantly and I had to tell him when to stop at each meal. He showed too little initiative. There were so many things wrong that sometimes I would despair that I could ever make progress and then, of course, we would make a new forward. It was just like the dark before the dawn.

He seemed far too unaware of his own self, which was not surprising, and far too lacking in emotions. If his feet were wet through, for an example, he would not know this, even when questioned, and asked to think about it. At times I smacked him, but he would cry only for a moment while it hurt, and not because he was angry or upset.

And if I punished him, he would accept it quite coolly without any feeling. Once I was crying bitterly while I was holding Jeremy in my arms, and he was quite unaware of this until the children told him.

But for months I made sure that, as far as possible, I was always there, so that he had to turn to me for every need in an attempt to focus his eyes in the natural way on to one single person.

I got very angry at times, and I noticed that for some months all our emotions were far too strong. In turn, I could see that each of us went through a period of intense hate and I watched its pain until it gradually died away. Oh what a blessing it was to feel the peace again. And always I was watching to see that at no time would a single personality get broken.

Sometimes in a desperate patch, we would be unjust to Jeremy and feel guilty, but life had to be faced and lived through in its entirety, the good parts and the bad – we could not run away from life. One day I heard Peter ask vehemently, "Why did you come here anyway?"

"Because Mummy wanted an adopted boy," replied Jeremy. I was proud that he had been able to deal with the situation so adequately.

And later, Peter asked me, "Mummy, why did you adopt Jeremy?"

"Because I wanted to." He seemed able to understand completely that it was to fulfil something in myself, and was at peace.

It was so like the birth of a natural baby in some ways. The intensity of emotion, and the adjustment to a new way of life, and gradually, as the days slipped one into the next, the newness wore off, things improved and everyone settled down. The intense consciousness faded away with its endless hurts, and the peace, the blissful peace of forgetfulness, replaced the trauma.

5

All these "high emotions" were alright, but still the work had to go on! Biscuits had to be made, a great tin-full, of which we were all very proud. The recipe was excellent and so easy and made 2.5 lbs of biscuits.

1 1b. Plain Flour
(Prewetts Flour from the Health Food shops is the best I think, and is free from added chemicals.)
1 level teaspoon of Bicarbonate of Soda
0.5 oz. Ground Ginger
Mix all ingredients together.
0.5 1b. Butter or margarine
1 1b. Soft Brown Sugar
1 egg

The butter and half the sugar are creamed together and the rest of the sugar and the beaten egg are added. Add the dry ingredients. Knead a little and make into small balls the size of walnuts. Put these onto a greased and floured tin and cook for about 20 minutes at Reg. 4.

Of course, other spices can also be added – nutmeg and cinnamon too, which make a delicious spice biscuit.

Were all boys a bit absent minded I wondered? Peter got up one night to spend a penny, came and stood right by my side of our bed and started to wee all over my blankets. I screamed at him, "It's not the toilet – it's Mummy's bed."

"No, it's the toilet," he mumbled, as I leapt out of bed and bundled him, protesting, towards the bathroom.

Louise made us smile too. She had been blowing up a tiny red balloon, when suddenly she swallowed it. It went straight down with no sign of choking, so I was not worried and thought that, given a little time, it must surely come through. So I asked her always use her potty for a few days so that I could check for the balloon. But no balloon appeared. I was wondering what to do next when the following morning I heard a very little puff-puff. I went upstairs, and, sure enough, it looked just like that little red balloon.

"Where did you get it, darling?" I asked.

"It's alright Mummy," said Louise, "I washed it foroughly."

The sales were on, and once or twice I had been to look around. In one shop I saw a china tea service and dinner service in the sale which I quite liked, and so Matthew's Mother left us when she died and we wanted to buy a dinner service so that we could remember her with it for a long time to come.

Several days went by while we thought about it – it seemed that Matthew still had his mind on another one, but finally I was able to persuade him that we should buy this china service for twelve people.

So, at last, quite convinced, he went down to say that we would have it, wondering if it might have gone. But we were lucky and it was to be ours. We were so thrilled as we undid each piece that night and examined them to see why they were put out as imperfect. Matthew's Mother always did love a bargain!

Great excitement – Matthew was invited to play a game of rugger. He was so thrilled to be asked again and very amused to discover that he was at least ten years older than most of the others! Poor old man! But he redeemed his many years by scoring a try. That really made his day. Needless to say, he spent the whole of the next week nursing his bruises and consoling his ageing musculature!

Quite close to our house, there were lots of blackberries and they were such a joy to pick and bottle for the winter pies or make into blackberry and apple jelly. For bottling them, I used the dry method, filling the jars with washed blackberries and pouring boiling water onto the fruit. The tops were put on loosely and the jars placed in the oven (on newspaper) for about 20 minutes at Reg. 4. I then took them out and tightened the metal screw tops and left them to cool. The exciting part was the following morning when the time came to test them. The screw tops were removed, and if the fruit had sealed, the jar could be lifted by the glass top only. Success – five had sealed and one had not, so we could have the latter as blackberry ice creams.

This I made by liquidising the blackberries with some soft brown sugar. Then this and a carton of double cream were stirred together in a bowl and put into the freezing compartment of the fridge on a cold setting. The ice cream needed stirring with a fork about twice during its freezing and really was delicious, and it seemed to go so much further than bought ice cream.

Jeremy still ailed with his chest and it was never really clear, and each time the Child Care Officer came, he seemed to be coughing violently or I had kept him in bed. I could not get him really well. He was often wet, every day at some time! If he played with boats, water would be all over his feet. When his pants were wet, he was ashamed and did not tell me, and so he stayed soaked until I had discovered him! At night he was still wet from time to time, not damp, but saturated several times, and slept in the pool of wetness to wake cold and sneezing.

It was so embarrassing – I was sure that the Child Care Officer felt me to be totally inadequate. I can remember that once she remarked that "Your children never wear shoes." It sounded so feeble when, in my own defence, I tried to explain that I insisted that the children wore shoes on all but really hot days, but that they themselves regularly took off their shoes and left them all around, making it difficult for me to find them. The fact that they were always barefoot and/or wet and/or muddy did not help me to convince her!

The doctor called one morning to see Jeremy and asked to talk to me privately. We locked ourselves in the only room with a lock to have a moment's peace, and he told me that he had been asked to tell me some bad news.

"You are to send Jeremy back to the nursery," he said gently.

I was flabbergasted. "You can't be serious!" I said."The child is only ill. We will get him right in the end."

"You have bitten off more than you can chew." And he left. I was left devastated and so angry and upset. If Jeremy went, that would be the end, for I could not start again. This was something I had never for a moment considered. From the beginning I had held it in reserve that if it was truly too much, for any one of us, Jeremy would tragically have to go back, but I had never for a moment thought that they would take him back unless his mother wanted him. Although this was clearly printed on all the forms, I had felt that it was not likely to happen and now it had happened. I just cried and cried.

"Why are you crying, Mummy?" asked the children.

"Because Jeremy is always ill and never stays well," I replied and I did not tell them any more.

Matthew was brilliant at handling people and without his ability throughout that whole period, there would, I have no doubt, been no little Jeremy in our family. I told him the news that night and he decided what to do. He guessed that in Head Office the decision had already been made to take Jeremy back, and he knew he had to tread softly.

He spoke long and gently with the Boarding-Out Officer whose ultimate decision it was, and asked him just to consider allowing us and them together to take Jeremy to see a private chest specialist of their own choosing. (We had already seen two different doctors, an Ear, Nose and Throat specialist, and had X rays taken but with no benefit.)

The following day Matthew phoned again and we were granted a reprieve and an appointment was made to see an eminent chest specialist, privately.

My resolve was intensified. I just had to get him well before we saw the specialist, to prove that it was not psychological and that I was not entirely incompetent!

So – water in every room was banned! I potted him hourly through the day and two hourly through the night to keep him dry. From the doctor we obtained a double dose of penicillin – to give him ten days continuous supply, and I pulled out the last trick of my trade. Very, very deep postural drainage, to get every spot of residual mucus from his chest.

It worked. He became completely well, for the first time for months and stayed well for one whole month! During which time, we saw the specialist, who clearly thought we were all slightly crazy, bringing an entirely healthy child to see him.

Only now with Jeremy in our family I knew why I had wanted an older child and had jibbed when the adoption society had suggested a baby. I realised I had "gone past" babies. Jackie was nine and a quarter years old, Peter six and three-quarters, Rosemary four and three-quarters, Jeremy three and three-quarters and Louise just two. For the first time in ten years, we had no nappies, no feeding bottles, and we were free to get into the car and go out for a picnic without leaving a baby with a neighbour first.

As a family, we were beginning to grow up!

Settling Down

1

For a long time now, we had been looking for a bigger house, for though we loved our bungalow, it had only one living room and three small bedrooms. Matthew and I shared the small double room with Louise; Peter, Jeremy and Rosemary had the larger double room, and Jackie had the tiny bedroom, and although we coped marvellously, there was not an inch to spare. We had even bought our old farm cart with the idea of making an extra room on it, rather like an old gypsy caravan, to spread ourselves.

Now with Jeremy's chest having proved tricky, and Peter almost seven and wanting some privacy, the need for a bigger house became desperate and after much searching, we found a large house in an adjacent village.

It was a fabulous house for us, and we called it "Deersleap". It had a garden large enough to grow vegetables, old established fruit trees, and six bedrooms, lounge, kitchen, dining room, and a room that could become a laundry.

We were overjoyed. It was on the edge of Ashdown Forest, a beautiful, carefree part of Sussex, and up a cul-de-sac, where the children would be free to run in safety.

There was so much work to do! We had scraped together just enough money to move in, and to do the most essential work, leaving much to do over the years to come. Matthew built cupboards, laid floors, made a fireplace, built walls, fixed ceilings, and worked so hard through all his spare hours, and it made a splendid home. At last we really had space.

Matthew and I had a room to ourselves, Jackie, Peter, and Jeremy had a room each; Rosemary and Louise shared a pretty room together, and into our spare room we took two students as lodgers, to supplement the finances. This was a help, for I knew that we would need this money. They each paid me £2.10.0. a week (compared with the 35/- a week I received for Jeremy) which included just their room, heating and lighting, bathing and ironing facilities. They ate all their meals at the college. Of course we often had cups of coffee together and when they were ill, I fed them frequent nourishing meals – free – to encourage them to get better quickly!

We now needed to buy Jeremy his own bed as he had slept on Louise's bed and Louise slept on a camp bed, and so we bought him an inexpensive divan bed and a white wood chest of drawers of his own, which looked lovely when it was painted with three coats of clear polyurethane. I do not think it is realised that just equipping a child out with bed, bedding and chest costs so much. One can always get things secondhand, but somehow for a small child I felt things should be clean and fresh.

So we settled in for the winter, very glad to have space, and very happy to have our lovely home in those beautiful surroundings.

The children were funny about moving and the young ones would ask if they should pack up their toys again, ready for the next house. Moving was just something that people do quite often, they thought!

Soon after we moved, a man called at the door, looking very grave indeed. "Matthew has had an accident," he said.

"Is he badly hurt?" I asked.

"Yes, I think so," he replied.

There was no-one whom I knew to look after the children, so I asked if his wife was free and would take them. He said she would, and so after noting his address, and washing three grubby little faces, and explaining what was happening, I dispatched them off.

I felt so cold inside and drove quickly to the local hospital, glad that it was a marvellous hospital and well used to serious cases.

After a while, I found Matthew, lying very flat and still on the trolley, his head and neck firmly sandbagged. "Hullo, darling," he said without moving.

"Hullo," I said. "And what do you think you have been doing?"

"A lorry ran into the car at a T-junction. I think my neck has gone." He could move his feet and his hands, and they had been careful in moving him to the X ray department to keep him as still as possible. The X rays had been taken through the trolley in order not to move him. An hour had passed since the accident.

I wandered back to the casualty department. Sister came towards me. "I have given him the best chance possible," she said gravely. "We have alerted Stoke Mandeville Hospital Spinal Injuries centre, and they are sending the helicopter to fetch him. We are waiting for the Radiologist to come and read his X rays."

I went over to the canteen to get a cup of tea, and be somewhere warm, for I was cold and shivering slightly from shock, and the bitter wind. This gave me time to take stock a bit. I knew what all this would probably involve. Matthew would almost certainly live, but would be probably be paralysed from his neck down, confined to a wheel chair and needing constant nursing care. Almost certainly, he would be unable to work or walk again.

But I was so glad he was alive. We would still have him around. I would have to earn the family income, doing work at home, but Matthew would still be there to talk to and we still had a Daddy in the family.

The time ticked by and I felt grateful that the man who took the children was slightly known to me. I learned later that he had seen the accident, and because he knew Matthew, he asked if he could come and break it gently to me, instead of the police giving me a greater shock. It was so kind of him to take the children, for I knew of no-one who could have taken them at the moment's notice and I needed to be free at this time.

I made my way back to the casualty department and, at that moment, our family doctor came in. Unknown to me, he had just seen the X ray report.

"Now, what do we do?" I asked.

"He's alright, just a whiplash injury," he asserted.

"What does that mean?" I asked.

"His neck is not broken, but just badly bruised from the fast movements of his head after the impact. It means that he is going to be alright," said the Doctor.

The realisation could hardly sink in for a moment. The gravity of those two fantastic hours were over.

"Sit up, Mr. Macdonald, and I will put a support on your neck," beamed Sister, so relaxed now and chattering gaily to the other staff. All the drama was over.

Matthew was all right and ten minutes later we walked, hand in hand, out of the casualty department, grateful for their immense care while they thought things were critical, and drove off to collect the children, very happy indeed to have Matthew still in one piece.

3

Jeremy continued to become more normal all the time and the days were often uneventful. Still we had occasional bursts of antipathy, brought on I think by my attitude, for children are so quick to sense how one feels. When Jeremy behaved in an unnatural way, I reacted and then everyone felt furious and hated him for being there. But on the whole, we got through those first months without too much family upheaval, not too much hate, nor too much love, but just about the normal interplay in the family. And how grateful I was for the other lovely children who came around to play, and gave us all the much needed diversion, and a dilution of our emotions.

Things improved only slowly of course, for Spring does not burst in a day, and only now and then did we realise that we were winning. One day, Jeremy and Louise were playing mothers and fathers, and Jeremy went off to 'business', and insisted that Louise should stay at home and look after the babies! It was the first time I had heard him playing mothers and fathers and my heart leapt for joy. We were one step further on in the understanding of reality.

One day, in town on my own, I met Anita from the nursery, that little girl for whom I felt so much. She was with one of the nurses and looked so lost – just three years old and so lovely, and still – nobody's child. Inside I just wept and prayed that soon her own Mummy would come.

"Nobody's child has far to go…alone"…I felt that should be added to that rhyme.

There was a spell of snow later and everywhere looked beautiful, and refreshed. The snow was so white and the trees were all edged with shimmers of silver, under the clear blue sky. The older children had little sledges that Matthew made for them and they used to pull the younger ones, all looking gay in their bright colours in the sunshine. The sledges were painted red, and blue too. It was a job keeping the young ones warm, but one tip that has been successful was to put a pair of Daddy's socks right over the outside of the young children's boots, then the snow cannot get inside to wet their little feet.

The children often played outside in their spare moments and went out one morning to find all their sledges gone. Stolen in the night. What disappointment and tears, and how angry one felt – we liked our sledges so much.

4

Our house was in a friendly village and quickly we were assimilated into its life. People seemed to be so warm hearted and, even in the 1960s, life still revolved largely around the church and its many activities. At Easter, four hundred people took Communion at the village church, out of a population of four thousand. There were also in the village three other denominations, so one can imagine the large number of people who took some active part in the Easter festival and found it had some real meaning.

We were rather amused by the story of a father in the village who had given his daughter a lovely wedding, and on the door of his shop he had placed a small notice explaining. "We are closed for my daughter's wedding. Please come back on Monday – I shall need you then!"

The students had settled in well; they were American girls, both from American Universities, who had come here to try to escape the whirl they had found over there, and to try and find significance in life for themselves.

We too had settled in well, but I do not think the Child Care Officer used to realise how well, when she saw so much of our house unfinished. But in time, we would do everything and get really ship-shape.

Already, I was aware that we were running into trouble financially, and I did not seem able to economise further. We had no papers, we did not smoke, Matthew and I had so few clothes and my domestic help came for only two and a half hours a week. I tried to start a playgroup in my own home and was turned down by the Planning Department of the local Council as being "detrimental to the amenities of the existing dwellings in the locality"! How ironic, when very often there were ten or more children playing in the house or garden. There was no playgroup in the village, and the parents had demonstrated the need to me and applied to come. One child lived in a caravan, three children were taken to work with their mothers, four were very isolated from other local children, one's mother was unmarried and one was recommended by a specialist as a prelude to starting school. Two or three more mothers just wanted their children to join in the fun of a group activity. But that venture was not to be.

Gradually, I saw ourselves slipping more and more into debt, not a lot at first but sliding gently down the slope. Even with the small boarding-out allowance for Jeremy and with two students living in, I was not making ends meet and could not think how to do so. Jeremy was not at nursery school three mornings a week and this I felt benefited him and me enormously! Louise was two and a half and still at home.

So in desperation, once again, I told God just how much more money I needed each year, and committed our money problem to him. A verse in the Bible came to my mind – "My God shall supply all your needs..." and I wondered what an earth He would possibly think up this time.

It seems unbelievable, but a few weeks later Matthew was offered the job with his company that he had wanted for years, and left Sussex to work in the Midlands, with a slightly increased salary, but with the prospect that we would sell this house at a higher price than we might buy for in the Midlands.

So, exactly one year after moving into Deersleap, we packed up again and moved out, for the third time in three years, to an excellent family house in the Midlands. A house not to be compared with the one we had come from, but quite all right, and one which enabled us to bank just twice the amount of money I had suggested to God that day in prayer! Our mortgage stayed the same but now we had a little money to balance the books when we gathered too many bills.

I was sad to leave my beloved Sussex, but Matthew was very happy to have his new job and the children were happy. I missed the country though and the quality of life down there, and felt I would go back if ever I had the chance.

Strangely enough, this move was a benefit in another way, for we changed our Child Care Officer, and the children no longer realised that the charming lady who came for tea, and was so delightful with them, was an Official, and her visits caused no disruption in our family life. At least, not the first two. At the third one she saw Matthew, and together they reminded me of all the little events of the early days, which I noticed disturbed me a lot, and made me sharp with the children. I needed to have the whole thing settled and finished.

Jeremy felt troubled too, by the medical that he had to have, for every detail was again asked for, and that night he cried and cried in bed. When I talked to him I asked him "Why are you crying, darling?" as if I didn't know.

"I wish I'd been your born baby, Mummy."

"Yes, so do I, darling."

That night his bed was saturated again, after months of being almost dry. I felt so upset and worried in case I could not counteract what other people were doing to him.

This Child Care Officer said that she would press for the adoption to go ahead and that we would receive two visits two visits from the Local Authority Children's Department. I hoped that Child Care Officer would be tactful and not disrupting. Whenever we were reminded by the officials that Jeremy was different, I noticed that we were unwittingly a little tough on him, then it would pass away again. He bore it manfully but I wished that it did not have to happen.

It was now eighteen months since Jeremy joined our family, and in every way we were completely settled. There were no hurts, no troubles, and Jeremy was a normal, happy little boy who talked clearly, cried with sensitivity sometimes, and was usually dry at night. No more bitten nails, and he was doing well at school.

One day at school, his teacher was talking to me and showing me proudly the children's work. She was an exceptionally gifted teacher who believed that loving these young ones was the most important part of her work. As we looked at the pictures on the wall, she turned to me, quite forgetful to whom she was talking, and spoke about the child. "This one belongs to a child who a year ago was emotionally disturbed, he'd lost his parents and his family, everything. Look at it – so composed and balanced."

"That's the picture of a normal child," I said.

Neither of us had noticed the name at the top of the picture, my child's name!

6

At this time, I read a very old book called "Life in my Hands" by Wally Thomas. It moved me tremendously, and gave me many hours of unexpected riotous laughter and poignant reading.

Wally Thomas was twenty at the end of the war, when he was severely injured, and lost his sight and hearing. One can hardly imagine just what it must mean to lose all normal contact with the people around. Each handicap alone is bad enough but to be faced with both together at that age, and for a young man who was so fit and with such promise ahead of him.

It has been said by Wally Thomas that a new situation must be followed by *Acceptance*, and *Adjustment* and the *Achievement*, and how much disabled, ill, or different people need the help of all the rest of us to be able to go from acceptance of their trouble through the difficult period of adjustment, to a time when once again they are achieving satisfaction and a measure of fulfilment in their life. I think it was like this for us.

Wally Thomas's book is so funny. This was such a surprise to me, for one hardly expects to sit howling with laughter as one reads of his life. Through him, I learnt how to make contact with a person who is blind and deaf, by writing in capital letters on his hand to start with.

From there I learnt to write in the blind-deaf symbols which are much quicker. And conversation, which we normal people take for granted, is almost life itself to a blind-deaf person.

How humbling it is, as we grumble our way through a bad wash day, to listen to Wally Thomas saying: "With gratitude there can be no bitterness." And for someone living in what must have been the very worst of suffering.

After all efforts to restore his sight and hearing fail he writes: "We have God in our house but we don't often talk about Him. I don't think He's there just to be talked about. Friendship with Him can become extremely complicated if one accepts the fashion of worship that has brought in its train the rules and regulations, the formalities and pomp and circumstances that have to my mind tended to cloud this simple and supreme issue, the pure possession of a faith."

Yes, in the religious turmoil that some thinking people are finding in the organised Churches, we must all desperately try to find true religion. We must try to understand what Christ was really like, and then use all our imagination and humour to put His life into practice in every corner of our lives.

One thing all Christians are sure of (one of the few things!) is that we can have the Holy Spirit, the Spirit of God which works silently through us. In this way God himself can work in us.

But, of course, only if we want Him to be a part of our life. Even if we do not understand but just want it, we can pray:

"Please God, come into our lives."

And then:

"Please God, take us on from there."

God longs to be our "very best friend" as the children would say, if only we would give him the chance.

Sometimes, even if we are convinced as Christians, the rush of life and the utter idiocy we sometimes find in our church services, clouds our images of Christ and makes us imperceptive, but if sometimes we can take Communion, and sometimes sit down and pray, not using words but rather trusting that God is there and lifting ourselves, or people we are praying for, up to God, then amidst everything, we shall occasionally know for certain that God is there.

Church was comic this Sunday. First of all in the morning, I took four children to Morning Service, thinking that as it was Mothering Sunday we would be welcome! But no, Louise sang very nicely, albeit out of tune and very loudly, then thought that in a prayer, she ought to practice her whistling, all on a continuous high note. So when someone came and told me, very kindly, that the Family Service was at three o'clock that afternoon, I took the hint and we fled outside during the next hymn. It was so nice to be wanted!

But our last year's experience at another Church encouraged us to return, and return we did at the appointed time of three o'clock! This time in full force, all seven of us. A whole pewful!

Towards the end of the service, the vicar announced that the children could all go forward and receive a tiny bunch of flowers to give to their mothers. All our little lot trooped out and came back, each carrying a lovely posy of daffodils and greenery.

Full of smiles and with a kiss from each child, I was given each posy. I had, I am sure, the biggest bunch in the Church and felt very happy. Then I turned to Jeremy and gave him sixpence for the collection which was to follow, upon which he promptly disappeared and with an even bigger smile returned in a few moments with yet another bunch! "There's an eye for business," said Matthew with a wink.

I think it was the first time I had come home from Church having made a profit!

7

The Tibetans, I understand, think of their children as their jewels, and this is perhaps a little how we feel about them. That in each little person, there is a streak of gold, a little piece of God, which in a child can only grow into a strong mature person given love and a home in which to bide.

Jeremy was completely normal now, a fine little boy. On one occasion I was introducing all the children to someone who had not met them before. "And this is Jeremy," I said.

"And I'm adopted" he added proudly.

But still the legal adoption was not complete and until it was accomplished, we were all at a slight risk. I noticed that even the doctors were a bit cautious when they treated a foster child, because they too felt at risk. Repeatedly we asked if the adoption proceedings could be commenced and, at last, we were told that we were being transferred from the boarding-out committee to the adoption committee which, I understand, meant that we were, at least, proceeding in the right direction.

My parents were marvellous and very kind to all of us. We survived the patch which I thought would mean a complete break with my family and, at my father's suggestion, loved my mother through the agony. My mother really is a person in a million, for this was not easy for her, but she was fair and kind to all children and she was a person for whom two children were more than enough! Quite by accident, I discovered that she was so embarrassed by the size of our family that she did not tell any of her friends about our additions after our third baby! To strangers, she hastens to add that we are *not* Catholics!

We were all invited to a party one evening for the birthday of a very dear friend who, to our delight, was going to be Jeremy's Godfather. It was a very happy party and the children were delightful. "My goodness, where does Jeremy get his lovely dark hair and those soft brown eyes," asked a stranger. "Oh, that's what happens when you do it on a very dark night!" replied Matthew wickedly.

Our adjustment was complete. We were just delighted with our family and it was all so natural and easy. One of my tiny problems in the beginning had resolved itself. I had asked for a child older than Rosemary, who would not come between my two adjacent girls, for I was thrilled to have two children of the same next to each other, and always I felt sorry that Jeremy came between these two girls. I encouraged them to keep the special bond they felt for each other, but as they vied with each other to be Jeremy's best friend, and were jealous when he chose one rather than the other, it was at times rather difficult. Then they both decided to marry Jeremy! At last, he and Peter played boys' games together, cricket, football, cars and so on, which left Rosemary and Louise free to get on with being twinnies together!

Jeremy helped me out too in another respect. All our children were affectionate and warm, and so was Jeremy, and with Rosemary, Jeremy and Louise all within two and a half years of each other, they were all still young and very cuddly. But one mother cannot hold three hands at once or cuddle three small wiggly bodies at the same time. Bless his heart, Jeremy's generosity and sensitivity enabled him not to push himself in when Rosemary and Louise were cuddling but to wait his chance until he saw I was free. And I tried to give each child some special times when they knew for certain that by me they were just the tops and very precious to me.

Those days of trying to hold three little hands to go across the road are thankfully over. What does one do when the one little soul that did not get a hand simply lies down in the middle of the road and screams? It was a relief that they were all growing a little older and people told me that they were well adjusted children. I hoped so, and I hoped that each knew deep within himself that he was important and loved by Matthew and me, and out of this could develop self-respect.

8

Strangely, over the past two years, and in no way because of our own experience, three of our friends have tried to take older deprived children into their families but, sadly, with very different results from ourselves.

First we met Anona and Denis, charming, intelligent people with four children. Anona was a Maths. graduate, with a mature and normal mother, and she and Denis were practising Christians, Members of the Church of England. Anona had had three children close together and then six years later, "a little accident"came along, and as Anona was tied at home with this little girl, she wrote and asked an adoption society if they would consider placing an older child into her gap. But she never received any reply. (In my case, no written reply came, but, after six weeks, I had a phone call saying 'No'.) Why was not the request taken seriously, one wonders, if this letter was in fact ever received, for with her maturity and experience, she would have been very well equipped to do this work. As it was, she later wondered if they really could afford another child and went back to teach two mornings a week to earn just that few pounds that mean all the difference to the family between financial survival and debt. How easy it would have been for us to have taken the same path, if my impelling urge had not been so strong, or if Matthew had been less sensitive, or we had been a little more realistic about our ability to afford another child.

On moving to Deersleap, we had met a neighbour who had for years wanted a son and had landed up with four evenly spaced daughters, beautiful girls, the youngest being nine years old. Shirley had so much love to give and much to spare and they had, in fact, already brought up a friend's boy who had been abandoned by his parents and left with them as a young teenager. Now she wanted a real boy of their own whom she could adopt. Financially they were all right, as they worked hard in their own business and without any waste there was just enough money.

Shirley and John applied to a voluntary church society for an older boy and went through all the harrowing investigations that precede adoption, which they found, as I did too, quite an ordeal, but they were willing to do this if they could give a child a family and gain their own! But both Shirley and John, and Anona and Denis had decided to have no more babies of their own. For both couples, contraceptives would work!)

Things seemed to be going quite well and they were told that the little boy named Stuart, whom I knew at the nursery, had been suggested for them. Stuart was two then, a fine little boy and Shirley's joy and anticipation knew no bounds. She visited the nursery incognito, and took a peep at this small poppet, who as yet had never found anyone to call Mummy, and felt that she could love him into full vitality.

But it was not to be. Shirley and John were not church goers – to them it seemed a lot of mumbo-jumbo, and not related to the life that ordinary people lead. Not that they were anti-Christians, for their girls had been to a Church of England primary school, and then onto a Church of England Convent school. Each girl had her Bible by her bed and, in order to help to get Stuart into the family, she and John had had the three younger girls christened.

But, sadly, their application was turned down because, they were told, they did not get his Mummy and Daddy.

I felt so angry about this, for to me it all seemed so wrong, and I often felt that if Matthew had not been good at handling people, we would not have been able to get Jeremy into our family.

On moving to the Midlands, we met a very gay family at the children's school, and they never knew that Jeremy was an adopted child. Mary and Colin had four gorgeous young children and were likely to end up with a lot more, I felt, for Mary was still in her early thirties, loved her children round her and she and Colin were uninhibited Catholics. They had just enough money and often Mary had thought that she would love to share their abundant family with a child less fortunate. So when an advertisement appeared in their church magazine for a home for a small Anglo-Maltese boy, it seemed quite natural to them both for Mary to ring up the Priest in charge of the Orphanage and ask to be considered for this child.

To her absolute amazement, she was met with a tirade of abuse. With four lovely children she should be content and not asking for more, and anyway, she was surely making this gesture only so that she could feel good and noble inside! She was absolutely devastated and felt furiously that if that was how he felt, he could keep his bloody kids.

But these incidents do all make me wonder if they really wanted to find families for all those children who have no mother or do they really like keeping their children in Children's Homes.

Then I realised another peculiar case.

In one Sussex village lived a foster mother who took babies placed for adoption at birth, and kept them until the adoptive parents took them from her, acting as a short term Foster Mother for the County Council. She was wonderful with these babes who thrived and flourished in her care. Over the years, she had looked after about thirty-five babies, one of whom she took as a very difficult baby. Shaun had some defect and she was told that he might die and grew to be a fine little boy of two years old, loved by herself and her family.

Gradually she realised that Shaun was not going to be adopted, because of his defect, although this had improved, and so she applied to adopt him herself.

At this proposal, it seemed that there was a change in the attitude of the Council. She was totally unsuitable to adopt him, she was told and there were others wanting him.

I talked to this heart-broken person, who had been bitterly hurt by all this. Why, if she could care for him until now was she suddenly so unsuitable to adopt him, she reasoned? She was thirty-five years old, her own boys were nine and eleven, and all of them and the father loved the child and treated him as their own. And he had been placed for adoption as a baby. If others were wanting him, why had no one ever come forward to see the child? What she also realised was that to move this child now would perhaps break his small heart. He belonged into this family.

She was so upset by what was said to her and in the end she felt it must be that if she adopted this child, she would perhaps stop being a short-term Foster Mother for new babies, and the Council would be in a difficult predicament to replace her.

The sadness however seemed so unnecessary, when it should have been only joy. Is it official policy one wonders to discourage the adoption of the older children?

Family Life

1

We decided to visit the Specialist again about Jeremy's chest, for although he had stayed well since those first few months, he had never been quite perfect, and I still felt that something was wrong. He often had bronchial and nasal catarrh and was wheezy and breathless when he ran and played with the other children.

Over the months, three doctors had already seen him about his chest and we had seen an Ear, Nose and Throat specialist, but no one had been able to help us at all, nor had seemed especially interested. The Ear, Nose and Throat Specialist had been the most illuminating! After waiting a while, we were shown into his cubicle.

"Does it smell?" he asked me.

There was no indication of what 'it' referred to, and as there was nothing smelly about Jeremy, I replied "It does not smell."

"Does it smell?" he repeated.

"It does not smell." I replied again. And unbelievably, with those six words spoken , we were ushered out of his presence. It was all over. He had not looked at the child's ears, throat nor nose, or anything, I fancied! "We will write to your Doctor," I was informed. About what, one wondered!

But this time, we were going to an allergiologist, and after my earlier experiences, I decided to go privately and hoped that we would make some real progress.

This specialist spent nearly an hour talking to Jeremy, testing his chest, nose, general health and doing skin tests to find if an allergy existed. These and the X rays showed that Jeremy was intensely allergic to house dust and feathers. The mucous membrances of his nose were pale lilac, swollen and without the tiny hairs of a normal nose, and the specialist felt that the membranes of his chest would show similar changes. I might have guessed really for dust defeats me, and there seems to be dust everywhere in my house. I try, but I very rarely win!

But there were several pieces of good news. The specialist gave Jeremy a little machine to blow into and found that his breaths were of normal size. He was delighted, for this normal 'vital capacity' meant that the lung tissue was not scarred yet, in spite of the attacks of bronchitis and the bronchial catarrh.

We were to attack his allergy in several ways. Dust was to be eliminated from his bedroom. It has now been discovered that in the house dust lives a tiny mite, and it is this mite that causes the allergy troubles. His sheets and under blanket were to be laundered and his mattress vacuumed, each week, in order to get rid of all the dust in the bed. He was to use either a rubber pillow or no pillow at all, and no eiderdown, of course. The bedroom floor was to be wiped over each day.

He was always to have an antibiotic when he got even mild bronchitis to prevent scarring of the lungs, and a substance to inhale night and morning to prevent the allergic reaction of his nose and chest, and allow him to develop normally. We were to see the specialist again in two or three years. I was delighted and felt that we had really made progress this time.

Matthew had just finished dividing the girls' room and it was really successful. The original room was 13 feet 4 inches by 11 feet in size, with one large window and one large radiator along the 13 foot wall, and the division made two small delightful self-contained rooms for Rosemary and Louise. They were so pleased to have their own little dens, and we now had to stand outside and knock before entering. They both had a full length 2'6" wide bed, and a chest and a chair, and with a set of bookshelves, the rooms were most enchanting. They were both delighted to have their own corner of the house and the partition was so light and simple that it could be removed easily if we ever wanted to use the room as an ordinary double room again.

The first night in her own little "nest", Rosemary was in her element. She had had a little tea service given her for Christmas, and she invited all the children in for a cup of tea, biscuits and raisins and bits of cheese, and whatever else we could muster!

She was happier though, for she was nearly six and a half, and felt threatened when Louise spoiled her little things. And at last, her Teddy was able to get a good day's sleep while she was at school!

One weekend, we had some visitors to stay with us and it was a joy to see them. They were over here on a holiday from the States, their second visit since they emigrated in 1957. Debs was an old friend of mine and David was a scientist. And they left Britain after they got married in the hope of making a better life for themselves.

They had stayed with us on their last visit six years ago and that time, there was a total power failure in the whole district, so this time, we were doubly anxious to show them that our country was not entirely decadent, and that people here have been able to make some life for themselves!

We scrubbed and polished and cooked and prepared for their visit and by Saturday lunchtime, things looked grand. Everything was ready for their arrival, when the impossible happened. The entire drainage system blocked up!

I rang everyone I thought would be interested in our drains – the sewage department would come on Monday they told me gaily! The plumber came willingly but was unable to free the blockage, and finally, in desperation, Matthew made a siphoning overflow hose from the manhole to stop it flooding!

And so it was when Debs and Dave arrived – all of us looking clean and sparkling, the house impeccable, and the entire drainage system blocked. However, we had a lovely weekend, and we were delighted for them to meet Rosemary, Jeremy and Louise for the first time. Their two sons were fine boys of eight and eleven and the children had a grand time together.

But did we all laugh over our once again decadent Britain. Lights out the first time, and this time the lavatories!

The whole system was finally pumped clear after Debs and Dave had gone on the Monday and we found a missing dishcloth to be the culprit. Oh, Louise!

2

In the early days, there were two things that troubled Jeremy which I never told anyone about, and which eventually passed away completely.

One trouble was that his little "willy" was in almost constant erection, to the degree that it used to lie almost flat against his tummy. This meant that when he wet his bed, he was wet all over his little body, and when he wet his pants, his vest and shirt were soaked through.

I suppose that this was just the tension that he felt in his new way of life, for, by the end of a year, it had settled down completely.

The other thing was one of our biggest hurdles – telling the truth. He told so many untruths, not intentionally and not, I felt, because he was insecure, but because he seemed unable to think adequately for himself.

I suppose the thinking had largely been done for him at the nursery and he would be inclined to say whatever answer he thought was easiest, or whatever he thought you would like to hear. I would say to him, for example, "Go and put your boots on, darling" and he would come back barefoot. "Have you got your boots on, darling?"

"Yes, Mummy" would come the reply!

And if his boots were soaking wet inside, I would ask him "Are your boots wet inside?"

"No, Mummy" he would assure me with those big brown eyes!

During this same period, he was very absent-minded and lived in a dream world at times. I would tell him to go and get in the car and find that he had gone and got into the bath. It was harassing. He did not mean to be 'naughty' and this naughtiness arose because for a long time he did not realise that the simple phrases that were spoken to him had definite, specific meaning.

But gradually, and not without tears, he came to understand. He had to think for himself what was said to him, and think what the real answer was, and when he went to school eighteen months later, he could think with real responsibility and independence. It was lovely.

3

On one occasion, I was invited to a coffee morning in aid of "Shelter" organisation. It turned out that it was a fund raiser effort by a group of the local chapel.

"We are really the Young Wives," I was told. "And we have old wives too," chimed in a grandma from across the room.

"There's a midwives as well," added the Minister's wife, with a twinkle. "All shapes and sizes of us!"

For some reason, that reminded me of one time my mother and father came for lunch. It was a Sunday lunch, and we were all trying to be very well behaved. The pudding was delectable, and suddenly, one of the children shouted out, "Mummy, can we have sex?"

My mother's eyes met my father's.

"Yes, darlings, of course you can" I replied, hastily adding that it was 'secs' of pudding they wanted, nothing more alarming.

My parents did look relieved!

A visit to Derbyshire one Easter Monday was an outing which gave us all pleasure. The weather was perfect for early April with warm, bright sun, a clear blue sky and no wind at all, and the air tasted like wine. Everyone felt gay and smiling and soon we were packed up and into the car, plus two friends who were staying with us for a few days, to head for the off-the-beaten-track.

It took us just one and a half hours to find our spot, a quiet isolated lane sign-posted Back-of-Ecton, which took us to the top of the hill and there we parked, to breathe in the pure air and complete calm, so different from our home, where we could hear the life of the town roaring continuously in the background in the background through the day.

Our first job was to make our camp fire. We tried the old trick of rubbing two boy scouts together to light the fire, but without much success, so then we tried matches, paper and a fire lighter – with greater effect, and soon we were well away cooking our bacon, sausages and fried bread followed by bread and cheese, bananas and some Quality Street, until everyone seemed filled up.

The peace was refreshing, and after lunch, I lay for an hour, perfectly still, soaking in the stillness, while Matthew played football with the children.

The part we had chosen to stop in was typical of Derbyshire countryside with the houses built of local grey stone and dry stone walls edging the fields. We were in the Peak District National Park, a part of the National Trust lands, bleak country with scattered farms on the hillsides, and derelict houses, and a conspicuous lack of trees over the bare terrain. We noticed that the soil was absolutely perfect, a fine moist tilth, full of natural compost, and it felt wonderfully cool in one's fingers. We were in an area without mains electricity or piped water, and we found from a local farmer how the water was stored in meres, which were built of lime, mud and stone, to form huge pits which kept the water pure for drinking.

The stones revealed some flashes of beauty to us all, and we collected some marvellous ones with pinks and white and soft browns in among the grey. We found one or two tiny pieces which would make beautiful pendants, drilled with a hole and hung on a piece of leather thronging, and we all came home laden with stones large and small – to add more clutter to the house!

Our homeward journey took us past the River Manifold a very shallow river at that point as it flowed over the stones and boulders of the river bed, and we parked and spent an hour there. A tree had fallen across the river and made an exciting bridge for the children which could be bounced up and down if encouraged! It was still partially alive and great soft pussy willows had come out at one side. We collected a huge, beautiful bunch to grace our home when we got back, and after a long play in the river, and a cross country run to avoid the Bank holiday traffic, we finally got home, incredibly dirty, and wonderfully happy after our day out in the country.

4

I have recently written to some of the major adoption societies in London to ask for information about older children in their care who are, at present, living in nurseries or children's homes, and who are awaiting adoption, but I gained no useful information. None were ready to admit that there were children who were without families – yet I was not convinced. I feel that there are quite a number who fall through the net of a good adoption system, for various reasons. I wondered if a number of "difficult" children showed maladjustment which achieved a family of their own. Would we not all have been maladjusted in those same circumstances as children, I wondered?

This designation of maladjustment might be considered an adverse mental report and prevent them from being put out for adoption.

I felt certain that there were some parents throughout this country who would take these children as an important work to be done, and to do a useful job with them. What, after all, is the use of endless psychological help and child guidance, if the one thing that is needed is still lacking? A mother and a father of their own. What chance have the children in even the very best institutional care that this country can offer, of arriving at adulthood anything but inadequate, compared to people from normal families?

I thought of Shirley, whom I had met briefly in Sussex before we moved to the Midlands. A beautiful English child, tall and well bred, who had been moved six times before she was four. She went from her mother to a nursery at six weeks, from the nursery to adoptive parents at two, from them back into care at the age of three to stay with a kind child care officer whom she knew. Then she went back to another nursery, and from there to a children's home. By this time, she was three and a half and truly a child of misfortune, if ever there was one, and now appeared "maladjusted". Not surprisingly.

Then I thought of the boy, a little older than Jeremy and one of his nursery friends. He was almost four, and during that time in this one excellent nursery there had been three Matrons and three deputy Matrons, (two left soon after his arrival, the next two stayed for over three years and the last two came just before he left the nursery) all marvellous people but, nevertheless, different people. Even Jeremy who had been more fortunate than many in that he'd had one special nurse to give him individual care at the nursery, had had two different Matrons in charge.

As we grew to love Jeremy more and more, I realised how fortunate we were to have found him. It seemed like a miracle to me sometimes – for we were only in Sussex for three years, just long enough to have discovered him and absorbed him into our family. Just in time too to prevent him from being moved to an older children's home, another probably final move in his little life.

Strangely, it seems to me that if I had simply applied to the adoption societies for an older child, I think we would not have been successful. We loved him so very much and, after all these months, I felt the same joy in him as I had felt about the other children. I loved him and I just thought him a wonderful person, whose company delighted me.

Gone for good, I hoped, were those feelings of guilt that I used to have at not feeling quite the same about Jeremy as I felt about the others. We just loved him, and perhaps more important, liked him immensely.

I had always believed that for some people at any rate, love is something which grows rather than happens. Certainly it was that way for me. When my babies were born, I did not feel love flowing through the room, but it grew in tending and looking after the child, and so it was with Jeremy. Gradually, through caring for him, our love had grown until it was something big and wonderful and quite natural.

5

It troubles me continuously that there are some children whose family contact has irrevocably broken down, and who, for various reasons, stay in children's homes, until they are thrown later into the wide and wicked world, in many ways emotionally quite unprepared.

Staff change in even the best nurseries and family group children's homes, and so with the best will in the world, they could never offer the continuity of relationships that a child needs to develop normally and counteract the tragedy of being uprooted and let down in their early life.

Those children who by parental wish or due to desertion are available for adoption, could be taken into families for life, and families who wanted to do this long-term fostering could be paid the full cost of keeping a child, about six guineas per week on 1970 prices, plus four pounds fifteen shillings per week for doing this work. (This is a salary which is just below the £255 per year that a married woman is allowed to earn tax free after the 1969 Budget. It costs between £16 and £20 per week to keep each child in a children's home, so this still gives a good saving of money spent.)

We are in a period when many wives are returning to part-time work, to earn a small amount of money for the family, and wives who wanted to make it their life work to care for a deprived child in the normal environment of a family could be enabled to do so.

I feel certain that there are some people who long to do this work and whose expertise in rearing their own children first would give them the skill and experience to help these difficult children very well indeed.

Many families now use contraceptives successfully to have just the number of children they feel they can afford, when truly they would love to have more, and so these families could be used to give really normal family life to deprived children and the chance of friendship with these parents, lasting through childhood, into adolescence and right on to adulthood and perhaps lasting a lifetime, the natural way of things.

Nothing could ever be as good as the natural family for the child, but for a child who, for one reason or another, has failed to achieve adoption as a baby, this might be the best 'second-best' that could ever be offered them.

6

A favourite pastime has emerged over the last few weeks, called "Me, when I was born". I had to tell each child convincingly what it was like when he or she was born. How could I confess to them that I remember so little of the details that make such a yarn exciting and differentiate each story from the other?

Jeremy would whisper into my ear with a mouthful of wooshy whisper on these occasions, "Mummy, please tell about me at the nursery", and the children's delight at hearing this small yarn was infectious.

"Well," said I. "One day, a long time ago, we lived in Sussex."

"That's before God said we had to move," said one.

"Yes, that's it," I replied. "And in Sussex was a nursery rhyme for babies who didn't have a Mummy and Daddy to look after them."

"Jeremy didn't have a Mummy and Daddy," said Louise.

"That's right," I continued. "One day I went to visit the nursery, and spent a little time talking to the babies and children. One tiny, darling boy of two was hiding behind the nurse's apron." (At this point Jeremy always went into wiggles of delight.) "I persuaded him to come out. 'Would you like to play with my car keys, then you could pretend to drive a car?' I asked. He nodded and we found a place in the wall where my keys would fit and he played happily pretending to drive a car. When it was time for me to go, I asked this weeny boy for my keys, and kissed him and said I thought he was a gorgeous poppet."

It was our first encounter, and it was curious, for Jeremy was the first of the older children that I talked to at the nursery. Clearly the nursery had been a remarkable and happy time for him.

It was wonderful to see the Spring bursting through again in our town garden, and every day brought fresh delight as new buds broke into flower. Outside the lounge window huge bush of flowering current suddenly blossomed with a myriad of dark pink catkins, and the daffodils were ablaze with their yellow assurance of Springtime. There were tiny patches of primrose yellow saxefrage hanging from one wall and dark blue scillas covering the earth, making a sapphire carpet. The crocuses made a rich bowl of colour too, opening almost flat on bright sunny days to allow the tiny Spring insects to sip the nectar in their golden centres.

The roses were pruned at last, and we had made a start at clearing another vegetable patch ready for early lettuces. We had plenty of compost in this garden, for there was an abundance of leaf mould, and a pile of old chicken manure, and I was determined to give the children as many good compost grown vegetables as I could.

I was also fortunate in being able to get Allinsons wholemeal bread, to order, from my baker, which we found delicious, and more economical because we ate much less bread – it was more satisfying, I suppose.

Peter and I tried making our own bread using Prewetts compost grown 81% flour from the local Health Food shop and following the recipe on the bag. It was a marvellous success and we ate five large loaves in two days! I am certain that it was so scrumptious because Peter and I spent so long 'bashing the dough in'! (They call kneading in official circles.)

Farmhouse Bread

3lb. Old English Milestone Flour. 1oz. Yeast. (A pinch of sugar) 1 oz. Malted Fat (Lard). 0.5 oz Salt. 1.5 Pints of Water. (Milk in place of some of the water will improve the bread.)

METHOD: Place the fat in a tin on the stove to melt, the flour in a mixing bowl and the yeast and salt each in a separate breakfast-cup.

Take the 1.5 pints of water at just over blood-heat so that it feels comfortably hot to your hand. Pour some of this water over the salt and yeast in their respective cups and stir each with your finger until you can feel no more lumps. Now pour both, together with the remainder of the water, into a hole in the flour and mix all together for a few moments then add the melted fat, and work the whole to a smooth dough.

This must be covered with a cloth and placed in the warm by the stove. It is left to rise for 1 hour and then given a short kneading until it is firm clear dough as at first. Leave it again for 1 hour, knead again, and after leaving a further half-hour give the dough a final kneading and immediately divide it into loaves of the size required.

Mould the loaves under your hand to the right shape and place them in warm and slightly greased tins. Cover with a cloth and place the tins near the stove for the loaves to rise.

When fully risen (about 30-40 minutes), carefully set the tins in a REALLY HOT OVEN and bake for half an hour or more according to the size of the loaves. Turn the loaves out of the tins immediately they leave the oven.

A friend called the other morning with her children, and over lunch, she was talking about praying to Saints. She was a Catholic and so for her praying to the Saints was a part of her religion. "One Saint, St. Jude, is the Saint of hopeless cases," said Moira, "and always when I had exams as a girl, I felt that he was one person I could turn to."

"But you aren't a hopeless case," I said, laughing.

"I always felt hopeless then," replied Moira, "and I needed his help!"

Matthew had just learned a new card game and the other night we asked my Mother and Father to come round to play for an hour. Matthew taught the game and assured us continuously that it was uproariously funny, and that we should be laughing fit to burst after a short while. With poker faces we struggled on finding nothing funny whatever, until finally my Mother and I got the giggles because it was so 'un-funny'. We laughed and laughed until tears ran down our cheeks. It really wasn't a bit funny, but certainly he had made his point!

We were delighted to hear that Jackie had been awarded a

Grammar School place. We had the chance to state a preference for a Church of England school, and felt so fortunate that she was one of the few lucky ones to have a place.

She herself was pleased, for we had moved only six weeks before the exam and she thought she had no chance at all. I was glad, for she was certainly ready to be fully stretched and had worked so hard over the last few months, and her work had improved immensely.

How full of admiration I was too for the Education Department, that they could cope with the move onwards for all the children and still retain some choice for the parents.

7

Things had been going badly lately for me! It was the end of the Easter school holidays, and after seven long, grey months, Spring had wonderfully broken. But I felt gloomy, fed up and resentful. The children seemed to squabble continuously and I was convinced that I was the best loved Mother in the world, I don't think! The older children seemed to resent any discipline and help I asked them to give me, and Matthew was often away on business or at the office until late in the evening.

I felt furious with everyone and even their joy and exuberance annoyed me. I had not had a single day off since Louise was born, nearly four years ago! Oh, to be a man with evenings, weekends and proper paid holidays!

I grumbled continuously at Matthew and the children, all of whom I thought were unreasonable, and had to bully and threaten to get the tiniest job done. Not without justification – I felt certain – for everyone was impossible! I was convinced that I was most unsuitable for motherhood!

If it had not been for my dishwasher, I think I would have gone scatty! We got it secondhand for £7 from a newspaper advert a year ago and it really made all the difference to my life!

I noticed that they were preparing for the 1971 nationwide population Census, and was determined that the computer would record at least once that Mothers work ninety hours a week for no salary, with erratic overtime on top of this, and no holidays with pay or without pay!

But the more gloomy I became, the more gloomy I felt. I made excuses that everyone else was at fault and did not think that it could possibly be me, until I read a very impelling book by a missionary, called "Mighty Through God" in which she also found things not absolutely A.I, although on the surface everything looked all right.

She reminded me that sin, that old fashioned word was still around and had so many names today, a harsh word, a tight mouth, grumbles, our pride and unwillingness to give ourselves fully to our husbands, were just the sort of real sins that stopped the love of God flowing right out of us. We must come to the cross of Jesus each day and give our sins up to Him. This curious thing that we must do, I don't understand completely, and yet I do know that it works, that sin, which we cherish so lovingly, must be given away, for while we hang on to it, it blocks the power of Christ in our lives.

That extraordinary, strange law that we must be willing to die, so that Christ can live in us.

So, once again, I took my beastly family to God in prayer. But I also, and more important, took the beastly me to the Lord in prayer, and tried consciously to think of the sins I cherished best of all and gave them up to the Lord Jesus. I felt so miserable, and just asked Him to take each one of them, and put His Spirit in me instead.

Amazingly – even the next day, the children seemed nicer and instead of scowling and shouting rude abuse, they seemed to be smiling mischievously!

Each day I did the same again, trying to think each part of my proud self to the foot of the cross, and trying to project myself up to

God in prayer time.

It was strange, for though we had given ourselves to the Lord Jesus Christ, I had forgotten that important bit of spiritual law, that sin blocks Him from working in our lives day by day. How I longed for that true goodness that I have perceived in a few people; some Nuns I had met particularly seemed to have it, and I felt that perhaps I had spotted a real truth that would enable true goodness to grow in me a little more. I really hoped so.

8

Ali, our dear old friend from Sussex, had been to stay with us again, and it was such a joy to have him. He just sat and laughed at us all the time, enjoying the contrast with his usual quiet life on his own. He was full of sparkle as usual, and had a new piece of mischief this time. "You are an intelligent and well-educated girl, Di."

How disarming one can be! I felt so flattered that I could not perceive his roguishness. "What is the difference between illegal and unlawful?"

After such an introduction, I just had to discover the difference and racked my brains, but I could not work out the variation in the meanings. "I give up, Ali." I said.

"Well, I will tell you, Di," said Ali, beaming from ear to ear. "Unlawful is something against the government statute book. Ill eagle is a sick bird."

"Oh, Ali," I groaned.

He was on top form and went from strength to strength. "Did I tell you what happened the other night when Mrs. B. took me out for a run?" said Ali. I hadn't heard. "We were driving home after half a pint at the local pub and could see a police car behind us. We were driving very carefully when suddenly a hare darted into the road and sadly we hit it. It lay looking quite dead in the road. The police car stopped behind us and we felt certain that the policeman would ask us to take a breathalyzer test, but though he came towards us with a little black bag, he ignored us and went straight over to the hare. Taking out a syringe, he drew up some liquid, felt behind the hare's ear and gave an injection into its jugular vein. We stood and watched him, and after a few moments, the hare frisked up, raised one ear, then the other, saw us, and scuttled off into the hedgerow again. 'That's marvellous,' said I to the policeman, 'what did you give him?' It was hair restorer,' said the policeman."

Ali had taken me in utterly with his "true" story!

Time Passes

1

The wheels were moving again towards Jeremy's adoption and we received a very pleasant letter from the Society asking if we would go and have our adoption medicals to ascertain we were still in perfect health. I was delighted. It should have cost Matthew and me one and a half guineas each which would have been yet another unwelcome bill, but our N.H.S. doctor kindly agreed to do it for free. Adoption medicals are supposed to be paid for privately by the adopters.

We fixed the appointment for the following week, and after a looking-over, we were both pronounced still in good health, and the letter confirming this was sent off to the Adoption Secretary.

We started to search among our friends to find Godparents for Jeremy, for although he had been christened and named as a baby, we now had to find one Godmother and two Godfathers for him. That was not such an easy task as one might imagine, for even with Louise, our fourth child, we had difficulty, and now we had to find three more Godparents, making a total of fifteen in all. But we don't have that many close friends!

We had chosen our Godparents with a number of things in mind. We wanted someone to 'special' that child and be the only unshared 'Auntie' or 'Uncle' and we chose friends of ours who would, we hoped, be friends for life. We never asked the same person twice over and never asked a husband and wife in one family both to be Godparents. So that meant we'd had to find fifteen different families to befriend our children!

Our first inspiration was a beloved cousin, whose only son, a severely handicapped child died some years ago, a cousin whom I had loved since I was a child. We had not seen much of them since we both got married , and I had forgotten about him over the years when our families had moved to different parts of the country.

Then the families met up again and I found him just as lovable, and we decided to ask him to be Jeremy's Godfather. He wrote a most lovely letter back, but he and his wife already had three Godchildren each and they had decided some years ago not to take any more. They had already turned down a previous request, and with much regret and heart searching, he decided he could not accept Jeremy as a Godchild.

We'd had just this same problem with Louise's Godparents, so we knew it would not be easy.

One friend in Sussex had taken an enormous interest in everything to do with our getting Jeremy, and she had become a very dear friend, and to our delight, she accepted our invitation to become Jeremy's Godmother. So he gained one dear 'Auntie Yo' as his own special friend.

We had another dear friend called Jack, who at one time was Matthew's boss, but had now left the company. We had always wanted him to be a Godparent, but never felt it right while he was in business with Matthew. He was curiously a little like Jeremy, always smiling, and the same wonderful soft temperament, and he too agreed to become Jeremy's Godfather. We didn't know any other man who was still 'free' as yet to be his other Godfather, but we would keep our eyes open until we found a friend whom we would like to know for many years, and with whom the friendship looked as if it could be a maturing one.

We were talking with the children the other day about the folk who had come to the town from other countries.

"We have a lot of 'ees' in our School" said Peter. "There's a few

Chinese, and some Japanese, and a lot of dirty knees," he said grinning. "Do you know what I would call our family?" he continued. "We're the Lucknow Lunatics." Our address was Lucknow Avenue!

Later that evening, Jeremy, Peter and Rosemary were capering around just before bed in their almost-nothings, with pillowcases draped round bare bottoms to maintain their privacy. Suddenly I saw someone snatch one unwary covering away, leaving a young naked body scuttling for cover. "You look like a vulgar fraction," said Jackie, as Peter's bare torso hurtled past to the armchair.

Jeremy's chest had been wonderful since we saw the allergiologist, and he looked so fit with not a trace of nasal or bronchial catarrh, no trace of a cough, and no sign of a weak chest in any way. What a joy it was after all our worries.

We also noticed how at last Jeremy's initiative was growing, after being very lacking in the early days. That seemed to be almost the last effect of Jeremy's experiences that corrected itself, and I did all I could to encourage it. No longer did I say "Go and change your best jersey before you play in the mud, darling." Now it was "Jeremy, I shall be very cross if you play in the mud in your best jersey."

"I will go and change it, Mummy" he would reply.

The other day he threw a large stone onto the lawn.

"If that stone hits Daddy's mower blades, it will smash the machine, darling."

"Yes, Mummy," he replied, and so I repeated it again. "Oh, I will move it off Mummy." He had thought out the solution for himself, and acted upon it. I was so glad to see this developing in him.

He was so super and so clever with the other children. At his suggestion, he and Jackie had put a mirror on Louise's wall, by sticking a mirror tile at just the right height for her, surrounded with a piece of pretty wallpaper that he found.

He seemed to be an intelligent little boy and worked so well at school. There were many hurdles which we had to climb. Physically he had been stiff, knock-kneed, round backed, afraid of new movements, afraid of heights, and we had done many, many exercises and activities suitable for a small boy, until he became physically superb for his age, and, he told me, the second best runner in his class!

Mentally, most of the difficulties were associated with his not understanding the meaning of words. Counting was a big hurdle, and it took many, many months of games, songs and practices before he mastered counting up to ten. Colours were an enigma for a long time.

But, surprisingly, he could always concentrate very well, and had marvellous times when he was alone in bed. He also showed talent for art very early on, and painted and drew some very appealing pictures, surprisingly showing some perspective.

It was amazing how one's children seemed to be so talented, at such an early age too, even one's adopted children!

2

Louise was to start school in September, for although she was only four years old, she was desperate to go, and the nursery class at the children's school took the children from three years onwards. The teacher was most gifted with the children and they all seemed to love her and the school.

Jackie thought she ought to prepare her a little. "You must eat all your lunch, Louise," said Jackie. "At school they give you slugs to eat and potatoes with maggots in, and you have to eat everything."

"Do you really?" questioned Louise, very wide eyed. I winked at her in reassurance.

But what would I do with my last chick gone? Now, I would have no excuse not to get a job, and earn the few extra pennies which we needed. I did not look forward to going back to work again, for although I enjoyed my profession, I loved even more being a mother at home and would have enjoyed having time again to relax a little more and do the many things which got pushed aside.

I was reminded of a friend whose last child had gone off to school and the first day she felt quite desperate. "I must have another baby" she said. The second day, she felt better. "I must have a dog," she mused, and on the third day she thought, "I think it's...rather nice!"

The Voluntary Society Child Care Officer called again to check that our adoption medicals had been completed. She was lovely with the children. Jackie was at home a little off colour, and it was a joy to listen to them both in conversation, and watch Jackie warm up to the subjects. So few people could talk with a child of that age, and they spoke quite naturally together.

Louise was a bit miserable too, and a bit feeble with a very mild tummy germ, which seemed to linger around for a long time. Then we passed it on to Jeremy and then to Matthew before we got rid of it.

Occasionally, the memories of those early days with Jeremy came to mind. The Child Care Officer and I were talking about children getting burnt and it reminded me of the time when as a boy of nearly four, Jeremy had put his hand into the gas flame on the cooker. Not surprisingly, the children had been kept out of the kitchen at the Nursery while cooking was in progress, and so all those years had passed and he did not realise that the flame was hot nor that it would burn him.

He had also put his hand on the iron not knowing it to be hot, for again as might be expected, the Nursery ironing was done away from the children.

These gaps in his experience were difficult to overcome, for there had been so many gaps; so many areas in which his lack of the normal mother-baby relationship had left him without the experiences that are usually learned quite naturally and at the right time. I could see from time to time even now that things were learnt theoretically rather than through experience and experimentation. There is so much spontaneous experimenting in the life of a young child, which a well-organised, well-supervised Nursery may well rule out, on the grounds of cleanliness and order! And it is difficult to do the experiments at the wrong time. The inclination to do them passes, and when things are done at the wrong time, it all looks rather idiotic. Tipping one's bowl of porridge over one's head at fourteen months old is quite excellent, but at five and all ready to go to school, it looks a bit ridiculous!

Jeremy looked lovely in his school uniform, and he felt wonderful in it, so much so that he asked if he could have his photograph taken wearing it! To our delight, the portrait was excellent, and he really looked the radiant and lovely child that he was.

At last there was a portrait of each one of our children, Jeremy's replacing the little snap that had kept his end up with the others, until it was his turn to be done efficiently by the photographer. How pleased we all were to have it standing silently by all the others.

He was still a bit comical about getting up at night for the toilet. I had found that as long as I woke him each evening and sent him to the toilet, he remained constantly dry throughout the night. But he found it so difficult to wake up fully and would wander round the house dreamily on his guided way to the loo. One night he trundled downstairs (the bathroom was next to his bedroom) and stood for a long time in the hall, with his "willie" at the ready!

"Lift the seat, darling," I said to try to wake him a little more. He could not find the toilet seat anywhere!

He had been known to wee on my handbag, and one night he even had the presence of mind to lift the lid of the laundry box and spend-a-penny in that! He really was mystified when I asked him to pull the handle, and promptly settled for turning on the bathroom taps!

His school report was a joy. It said quite simply, "Jeremy has settled in happily and enjoys all activities. A start to reading has been made and Jeremy tried hard. Jeremy is a very friendly and pleasant little boy, always helpful and kind to other children."

How blessed we were that he was so settled with a school that suited him so well.

3

As the summer went on, we just rejoiced in the garden, for I loved gardening, and there were plenty of corners for the children's adventures. Matthew reminded me of one of our gardening antics in the earlier part of our marriage. We were, at the time, terribly broke after just moving house and so I answered an advertisement, taking on a job as a gardener at 5/- an hour. In my reply I did not tell them that at the time I was tremendously pregnant!

I was delighted. At last I had a job again. I felt certain that I could do the work while Matthew looked after the children. Fortunately for me, Matthew offered to do the job instead, and as a complete non gardener, it was a miracle! He was accepted.

He was still a willing labourer all these years later, while I fussed and nursed each little plant, hoping to rear it to a full size cabbage of lettuce before giving it to the slugs. Potatoes were my speciality. I felt that I had an advantage over the creatures with these, and last year I had kept the family fed on home-grown potatoes for two months.

But raspberries were really my pride and joy and defeated me completely, for in each house in which we had ever lived, I had dug and manured and staked out and planted canes, never yet to pick a raspberry! We always moved before they matured.

Jeremy too was very happy with the garden, but for a different reason. Long ago, we had given him a pass-on two-wheeler for a birthday, which he laboriously and not too courageously had learned to ride. But all winter, it had been badly punctured and at long last, Daddy had brought a new tyre and mended it. He jumped on it and with enormous pleasure, rode off without the slightest hesitation, all over the garden, down the slope, up the slope, on the lawn, and up and down the paths, just beaming from ear to ear. He loved his bike so much that for days he carried it up and down the paths, just beaming from ear to ear. He loved his bike so much that for days he carried it up and down his bedrooms for safety.

There was one other tiny thing about Jeremy, something which most people would not think important, but which I felt to be very much so.

He had always gone to sleep in an antenatal position, lying on his side with both knees drawn up rather high, and with his thumb firmly in, rubbing his tummy with the other hand until the skin became sore. I had always felt that a happy, secure child would often lie in other relaxed positions, and I had encouraged this and discouraged the thumb sucking and tummy rubbing. At last, after nearly two years with us, he could fall asleep naturally, in any position, and with no thumb in, and no tummy rubbing. He looked so peaceful, and very adorable, and so much more natural to me.

4

I have joined a tennis club again and on Thursday, I played my first set since we were married twelve years ago. My heart pounded, my head throbbed, my eyes blurred, but somehow I kept going. I thought I must surely have hardening of the arteries, and felt quite ninety years old. But what a splendid partner I must have had, for I survived, and we won. Perhaps next time, it would not be such a torment!

Recently, we have been adventuring into delicious salads again, and to my delight, the children all ate them with great relish. My special salads were compiled after we met an old retired doctor who was a vegetarian, and who talked convincingly about the immense value of fresh salads. So, in them I include grated Cheddar cheese, hard boiled egg, lettuce, celery, beetroot, cucumber, tomato, radish, grated carrot, cress, cold baked beans, cooked frozen peas, chopped parsley, orange, banana, grated apple, pear, dates, raisins, chopped walnuts, and a sprinkling of oats. It looks so pretty on the plate and very appetising, and if the lettuce is cut up fine, and each person's salad is made on a separate plate, it could be eaten with just a fork! Less washing up!

These salads need a potato salad served with them made with cold boiled old potatoes cut into small pieces, or cold mashed potato, to which was added chopped raw onion, chopped parsley, and a salad dressing of mayonnaise, cream off the milk, and lemon juice, salt, and paprika or pepper. This made a moist potato salad.

I used to make a special German dressing to pour on to the salad at the time of eating, which always seemed to add something very special, and being a sweet dressing, made the whole salad juicy and delicious, even to the young children.

It consisted of one egg yolk, mixed well with the strained juice of one lemon. To this was added half a cup of cold water and mixed well. A dessertspoonful of soft brown sugar was then added and it was all mixed again until well blended. The dressing was spooned on to the salad just before eating, and was especially delicious on the lettuce, grated carrot, tomatoes and cucumber. It will keep well in the fridge.

I had also been making rhubarb and ginger jam, with fresh rhubarb given me by a friend. It was growing abundantly in this early part of the summer in her garden. The recipe was as follows:

31bs. rhubarb (weight after cutting up)
31bs. soft brown sugar
3 teaspoons of powdered ginger
Juice of 3 lemons

The rhubarb was cut up into inch-long pieces and well washed, and stewed in a little water until tender. Then the ginger, sugar and lemon juice were added, and stirred until all the sugar had dissolved. Then I boiled the jam until it set. (To test for a set, I put a little of the jam on to a cold plate. When it was cold, I pushed one finger through the jam and I could see that a slight skin had formed, which meant that the jam would set if it was put into the pots.) The jam was poured into the pots and covered with the waxed jam pot discs, wax side down. I covered the jars a little later, and labelled them for the winter store cupboard. 51bs. more jam, full of nourishment and taste, at a cost of just a few pence per jar!

There was a portfolio growth of mint in the garden, and so apart from dispensing enormous bundles to neighbours, friends and relatives, it seemed a good idea to preserve some for next winter too.

I picked a great armful of the mint and stripped off the leaves, which I then washed well and chopped very finely indeed. I simply placed it in a screw-topped pickle jar, and covered it with vinegar, adding one good teaspoonful of brown sugar. It was labelled "Mint Sauce" and placed on the shelf to await roast lamb in the winter. How satisfying!

I have also learned to cook carrots without any extra water at all, and the result was the most delicious carrots I think I have ever tasted. I peeled the carrots and cut them roughly into small pieces, and then sprinkled them lightly with salt and Demerara sugar before putting them into a saucepan, to leave them for one hour.

The salt and sugar will bring out some of the water from the carrots themselves, and in so doing concentrate the flavour of the carrots. I then added a knob of butter and tightly fixed the lid on to the saucepan. Stew very gently, stirring occasionally, until the carrots are tender, and then serve scattered with freshly chopped parsley, or a white parsley sauce.

Jackie, our eldest daughter, was nearly eleven, and to her great delight she had been able to fulfil one of her long standing ambitions – to become an actress!

She joined a junior drama group, and was selected to play a small part in their production which was performed in a competitive festival. She did wonderfully well and was exactly correctly cast for her personality at the moment! She longed to progress into films or to get a chance to play on television, which seemed slightly less remote after my experience in a "Man Alive" programme on Playgroups in 1968.

Bath time was often a time for private talks and one night Jeremy sat in the warm water beaming and obviously feeling very pleased with himself. "Who do you really love best Mummy?" he asked.

"I'll never answer that darling, but I love you all very much and I love you specially a lot," I replied. "But who do you think I love best?" I continued.

"All the children," said Jeremy, "but me really the best."

That was just how I wanted everyone to feel.

Jeremy got the mumps from school, and suddenly grew very fat of face! We all went swimming towards the end of his mumps, and as he sat on the rug watching the others gambolling in the water, a little wistful voice lamented – "Mummy, how much did I cost when you got me from the nursery?" Jeremy asked.

"Nothing, darling. You can't actually buy babies these days. In the old days, they used to, but not any more."

That reminded us of when we sold the last house. We made a list of all the extras that we would sell if the purchasers wanted them, and at the bottom of the list we wrote very boldly: 5 children at 50p. each.

We had no offers! We just couldn't imagine why!

Another of those wonderful remarks came soon after, and my heart leapt with joy. "Mummy, I wish I could marry you" came Jeremy's voice as we walked back from the garden, our arms round each other.

"Yes, so do I, Jeremy," I replied. "I would love to marry you too.

But you have to choose someone who is not married already, and I am married to Daddy. But you will find the loveliest girl when you are grown up whom you can marry."

The moment passed, but what a wonderful moment it had been.

"Daddies have their value too," mused Matthew the other day, when Jeremy came to him, and asked him to make a hook for his breakdown lorry, something mothers could never do!

"Can I marry Daddy," Rosemary also asked one day. "I love him so much that I want to marry him more than anyone in the world."

It is indeed a blessing to have a Daddy, to love and to be around – to love as a man if you are a boy! It is all very special.

The Abandoned Ones

It is the summer,
The war struggles on
In Vietnam, A conflict continues,
A conflict no-one understands.

The babies don't understand,
Their father is dead,
Their mother is blind,
Her face pitted with shrapnel
From man's unique inventiveness.

The abandoned ones lie in the cots,
Three in each beds,
Three nurses to care for hundreds,
A bottle is propped in each mouth,
Some suck, others lose their bottle
And it drips on their clothes.
Some die, but the strong ones survive.

Now they are older, in the perfection of babyhood.
They sit
Motionless,
Not hearing or seeing, or crawling or chuckling,
They are dead inside –
The unwanted ones.

6

I heard a most wonderful programme the other day on B.B.C. "Woman's Hour", and it really seemed like a ray of sunshine in a sometimes dark world.

A vicar was talking about an enterprise started by himself, and accomplished through prayer and the guidance of the Holy Spirit which he called, I think, Project Vietnamese Orphans. The idea was to bring twenty orphans from Vietnam to England to be adopted, and so far five had been settled over here, and three more were waiting for documents to be finalised.

One particularly wonderful story thrilled me. It might have been called "Miracles Still Happen". Apparently among the first babies to be brought over to this country was a pair of twin boys, one of whom was stone deaf. The adopting family were very apprehensive about raising a stone deaf child, but decided to go ahead. Incredibly, the miracle happened. After three weeks with the new parents, three weeks of being loved and fussed and cuddled, the chid could hear. He had cut off his hearing himself, when life was no longer worth living and he found that no-one loved him, and now that life was really worth while once more he could hear again perfectly, to the joy of the family. What rejoicing there must have been.

The plight of the babies that remained was grim, but there were many offers of homes for these children, and only so few could be brought to gain a new chance in life.

One so often forgets one aspect of the aftermath of war – the huge number of mixed race children conceived by people seeking perhaps just human warmth in the midst of an inhuman affair. In the case of Vietnam, there are, of course, numbers of American-Vietnamese babies, who belong to neither group, and whose parents will almost inevitably be separated from each other by their day to day existence of war.

7

The summer was here and we had decided to try to get some sunshine for our summer holiday, and with very great saving up, we had our tickets to France, and an apartment in a North Brittany seaside town. The preparations had been made, including our passports, and the children's minds, to the concept of leaving our island for a brief spell and visiting a foreign country!

We had to write to the adoption Society for a passport for Jeremy, and how I wished that he was legally our child, so that his name could just go on Matthew's passport with all the other children. He still had to have a separate passport. I had received a letter back saying that this was being attended to, and that Jeremy's natural mother had first to sign the form.

That was the first mention ever made of her by official circles.

I felt scared. For supposing this made her think more about her child, so that when she was asked to sign the legal adoption form, which surely must be soon, she wanted him back.

For a long time after he came to us, for more than a year, I felt very much that she should have him back if she ever wanted him. I knew that during that time, she would become twenty one years old, and could no longer be made a ward of court, and might want her son back, even though she had not seen him since he went to the nursery at six weeks old. Throughout this period, I felt that if she wanted him

Jeremy, a year or so after he joined us

back, I could handle it myself, so that he could go back to her, to his rightful mother, without too much upheaval and upset in his young life.

But we had gone past that time, and now we thought of him as OUR child, with all that this really implied. He was a loved and belonging member of the family.

Was it possible, I wondered, that his mother might want him back now, when Jeremy was nearly six and after all these years?

How I wished that the judge had ruled all those years ago, that Jeremy's natural mother and father could have married without the consent of the parents, and given the little family a chance. How much heartache might have been spared had it been that way?

I had often wondered if it were God's will for us to have Jeremy. I wanted to do the will of God, and had prayed earnestly to do His will, but it seems to me that one can only see that things are part of God's plan in retrospect. I remember in that magnificent story of the Trapp family, portrayed in the film "The Sound of Music", that Maria is asked by the Reverend Mother what she had learned at the convent. She replied that it was to "find out what was the will of God and then do it". For her it had turned that the will of God was very different from what she had dreamed of. Instead of being a nun, she became a mother, inheriting seven lovely, but disturbed children, and then having several more of her own!

But what joy among the heartaches there must have been for her in doing the will of God, and what happiness they so obviously have found together.

Summer

1

The passport arrived safely with Jeremy's old surname on it. He was now our son in all but cold legal fact, and it was at moments like this that we were reminded that he was not ours and that, in law, we had no rights over him.

I still felt troubled that we might have problems at the customs, for all the other children were on Matthew's passport, so the Child Care Officer agreed to write a covering letter on official notepaper, explaining everything, in case we met with difficulties at the customs office.

With the holiday looming ahead, I was gardening in every spare moment, trying to be victor over feet high dock leaves and grass that looked like hay before mowing.

The vegetables were flourishing and Matthew had built me a cold frame. I was determined to rear lettuce from seed without the interference of slugs, and I think almost the whole packet of seeds must have germinated. With the glass top removed the sun streamed onto my tiny plants, and, to my horror, onto the cat too, whom I found soundly asleep lying comfortably on the lettuces in the cold frame!

Was it possible to win against all these adversities?

One of our projects in the garden was one which always thrilled me; we were once again building a compost heap. Mature compost is a natural way of adding enrichment to otherwise weary soil, and making it really fertile, and even a small garden has room for a compost heap tucked away somewhere out of sight, perhaps behind a piece of fencing.

Into my compost heap, I put the grass cuttings, hedge cuttings, leaves and all garden rubbish except nettle, ground elder, convolvulus, holly leaves and bramble. (Nettle, ground elder and convolvulus will spread through the compost heap from the roots, and the prickles of holly and bramble are a nuisance when handling the compost.) Soil can be added whenever there is some to spare, and all household refuse which has come from vegetables or animals is of special value, for in these are titbits for the birds coming from the kitchen.

I kept a special bucket under the kitchen sink to collect for my compost heap and into this went all the scraps from the plates, egg shells, and all the waste from fruit and vegetables. Of course, in nature there is really no "rubbish", for today's rubbish is converted into humus to enrich the ground for next year's crops.

So my heap grew steadily throughout the summer and when it was large enough, I stopped adding things to that one and started another one.

One cannot have too much compost, for in a year's time, when it is mature, I shall spread it thickly so that it covers all the soil, and then fork it in around my plants, and on my vegetable patch, before planting again in the spring.

One can see what a delight a compost heap is to the birds, for they are so often there, pecking at all the choice delicacies that come their way; that scrap of rice pudding, that half eaten fried egg, the stewed rhubarb that went mouldy, and so on. And in return, the birds add their droppings to the heap, providing some real old-fashioned animal manure – of a different kind, but none the less valuable!

It is surprising to find how much the soil is improved with the compost; flowers grow sturdier, vegetables are bigger and have more flavour, and the soil becomes wonderful to handle, as it becomes more fertile and enriched and full of life.

We unwittingly gained more beautiful flowers in our garden the other day.

My brother Richard brought round a most unusual plant from his family as a birthday gift for me. It was a Gloxinia, with its huge majestic leaves and enormous flowers like purple velvet trumpets. Gloxinia was to be lovingly cared for, I was told, and Richard told me how to water it, which I promised to do faithfully. Imagine my surprise the next morning, when I looked out of a window, to see Gloxinias entire contingent of blooms suddenly transported to the rockery.

Oh, Loo-Loo, how could I ever tell Uncle Richard what happened to Gloxinia? She looked so naked with just her leaves and stalks sitting all alone in the lounge, utterly flowerless.

We still had problems in our family. I suppose they will always be with us – we could never fin scissors, pencils or a comb! Are other families as bad I wondered? We have hung scissors on strings from nails, we have bought pencils and combs by the hundred throughout our marriage, and still it defeated us. Desperate one day, I offered the children a sixpence for anyone who found a comb so that we could tidy our hair to go out. Everyone searched feverishly in all the obvious places. At last a cry was heard – "I've got one" shouted Peter, handling me an almost entirely toothless comb, "only it isn't a comb, it's a prong!"

Which shoes did my little Rosemary go to school in on Monday? She was in the rare position of having two pairs of shoes and both of these were in her room, as were her slippers. Her gym shoes I knew were at school. Her Wellingtons were in the cloakroom. So what did she have on her feet to go to school? I hoped that she had not gone in a pair of my high heels. How ridiculous I would feel confronting her teacher!

Matthew often took the children to school on his way to business, and with him shouting furiously from the car, "Get in the car – Get in the CAR – Will everyone please GET IN THE CAR," it was a miracle that anyone ever got to school dressed in anything suitable! How can one explain to a six year old under those circumstances, that the dressing up clothes which were perfectly suitable for school in 1869, are not appropriate in 1969.

As the tension rose each morning, everyone was sure to disappear in the wrong direction to get their football, skipping rope, lunch money, hankerchief and homework, and Matthew got more and more steamed up, and more and more carbon monoxide fumes would pour out of the exhaust pipe and through the front door, making a conscious arrival at school even less likely!

At last, miraculously, everyone was in the car, still conscious, albeit I regret to say with shoes I know not of, and I usually staggered back to the kitchen to sip through at least two cups of coffee, and two toasts, and listen in a state of languid convalescence to Jack Demanio's soothing voice and await the recovery from the early morning.

Matthew and I were having problems in our sex lives too. He had a large and prickly moustache, and whiskers that grew with vigour, and making love was like making love to a raspberry cane.

I had tried to persuade him to shave in the evenings as well as the mornings, but he forgot, of course, or assured me that his skin was far too tender to stand such slaughter twice daily!

Our bed now is rather old too, and after years of twenty stone lying on it, it possessed a well defined trough right down the centre. Matthew always managed to get onto that comfy bit of the bed and I was left with what felt like the side of a precipice to sleep on, propped up by cushions to hold me from the much occupied crevasse down the middle.

I suppose double beds will always be difficult. It seems funny to think that some men spend all their lives designing big soft beds when all they really want to do is lie on small boney women.

Once, when our ardour happened blissfully to coincide (I have the old-fashioned idea that going to bed means going to sleep) we had such fun and laughter together that it was pure joy. "You are like a wild rhinoceros tonight," I teased Matthew. "You are supposed to be as gentle as a kitten with middle aged ladies." "But I get scared I'll have to wait until you are an old lady!" Matthew retorted, giggling wickedly. Oh dear, I knew my ardour had waned, but not that much I hoped.

We have discovered two new methods of contraception recently, ones which I have never read anywhere in those little books on the subject!

One was called the 'interruption' technique. Just as we were getting very, very friendly, in would come Louise or Rosemary for a little night-time cuddle.

Well, you can't refuse such a sweet idea, can you? The 'separation' technique consisted of a small girl having a walk to the toilet, after which she insisted on coming in between Mummy and Daddy, so that she could love both of us together! (She had a great sense of fairness.)

I will swear that it was the springs pronging on our bed that initiated those most effective forms of contraception. The results were invariably total non-alignment!

A voluntary children's society magazine came the other day, with a case history of one of its children included in its features. It was called "Too old at six months?" and it told of a premature English baby boy placed for adoption at birth, who, because he was small, had to wait for some months before he could be given a health clearance by the paediatrician. He spent that time in a nursery, when at six months old he was pronounced a fit and perfect child and ready for adoption. But being a boy and as old as six months, his chances of achieving adoption were said to be slim, for most people wanted new born babies, with twice as many girls as boys.

What a price to pay for being born a little smaller than the average. They told too of "a large number of genuinely friendless children" in the children's homes, and of their concern over this.

What a nightmare to grow up without friends.

Living in a normal family gives many friendships quite spontaneously, just through the normal contacts of the neighbourhood and school, and through the family activities.

One of the little incidents with Jeremy was included in their magazine. It told how Jeremy was placed in between Rosemary and Louise in our family, and then a short while later, both little girls decided to marry him. There was Linda down the road too, so he was doing rather well for a small boy of five!

2

The second year had passed and once again we were in debt. I still considered that it cost about six guineas each week to keep a child in a family, and our debt was just £330 this year, just about what it cost to keep Jeremy. We'd had to find a great deal of extra capital in the two years to pay for expenses directly incurred through having Jeremy – not clothes or food, but bedding, furniture, the bedroom floor, partition of a bedroom, private specialist and doctor's fees, his extra travelling expenses, presents to Jeremy, from him to us, an old bike, his teddy, savings I made for him, and so on (a list is shown in the appendix).

£180 was covered by payments for Jeremy by the Adoption Society from which he came who paid 35/- each week, which still left a deficit of £330 again this year. In our case, because of moving from Sussex to the Midland, we were able to pay off the debt and we had faith that we would cope in the future. But, with less faith and a little more financial prudence, might we not have done these sums before Jeremy came and turned down the idea, and so who knows, perhaps one more child might have grown up friendless, homeless, deprived, and unprepared for real life.

Many people must have thought of the idea, and sensibly said,

"We simply can't afford it."

It still seems to me illogical to keep any healthy child in a Children's Home costing about £18–£20 per week, knowing that at the best he will grow up terribly deprived (although this may not be obvious on the surface) when for about £10.10.0. a week (made up of £6.6.0 boarding payment plus £4.4.0 salary to the foster mother), a child could be raised in a family with the chance that he would be loved, and befriended, and treated as a normal person by the world in general. There is a chance too that he will be better prepared for the adult world in which he will have to live.

3

The day before our holiday had arrived, and all was ready. We had borrowed baggage, so we had one case each – seven little cases in all and Matthew came home from business, and demanded a dress rehearsal for packing the car, so there we stood all queuing up to load our cases into the boot, with Matthew using his imagination to fit all the other things in too.

Miraculously, next day, everything did actually get packed, two camp beds, bedding, sheets, towels galore, tins filled with cakes and biscuits, butter, squash, pillows, games, groundsheet, and every small commodity that someone was certain that we would be sure to need – sun hats, sun lotion, a picnic and so it went on.

The preparation had gone on for days it seemed. I packed the children's small cases – they repacked them with what they thought they should take. I felt frustrated. This time I had no intention of taking panda, and brown bear, and golly, and dolly and woofer and all the other creatures that comprise the family, but every time I looked at the pile to be taken, there they all were again.

It was a long day waiting for Matthew to finish business, the house was clean and tidy, the never-ending pile of ironing had, for once, disappeared, and we were all fed and just waiting. At last a honk-honk was heard and the car rounded into our drive, with Matthew beaming and looking as fresh as ever. It was 4.20 p.m. Matthew was like a magician. He packed the boot with not an inch to spare, and not a thing left behind that he wanted, and by 5.20 p.m. we had gone, sadly leaving pussy for two weeks to a neighbour's care.

But Matthew's smile faded. "We are twenty minutes too late leaving," he grumbled. "Now *all* the traffic will be in our way." But mercifully it managed to keep moving on our side of the road, and we kept going too, so that crisis passed!

Being a mere woman, I have never felt the impact of the swarms of cars that invade the roads at certain times of the day, and have never fully appreciated the geometry of passing through certain major points at certain specific times, BEFORE everyone else thinks to go that way.

This journey was going to be a long, hard trek I thought, for the first spell by car would take us about five and a half hours, arriving at Newhaven about 11.00 p.m., in time to catch the 11.45 p.m boat to France. But everyone was wonderful, no doubt keyed up by the adventure. And surprisingly, no-one even nodded off to sleep. We had hit upon a new seating strategy this time, for Matthew had two children in the front, and I sat in the back of the car with three children. This way child energy was slightly more hampered by adult repression than usual, which we thought might be a good thing!

We arrived at Newhaven in good time, at about 11.0 p.m., and had time to stretch our legs and visit the toilets before going through passport checks which presented no problems. The officer just counted the children and asked who Jeremy was, seeing that he was being adopted by us, and that was all.

It was a French vessel, and we drove on to the boat to spin round on the turntable to face the outgoing way, and parked neatly like sardines, all ready for disembarkation.

Fortunately, we were able to get six seats, for the boat was filling up fast. Six seats which were perfectly fine while we all sat upright, but soon, Louise was asleep, and Jeremy, and Rosemary, and as they were sitting we thought they would fall off, so we curled them into tight little balls and laid them down. Jackie and I went off to have supper – a delicious French meal of chicken in a rich sauce and potato crisps covered with the sauce, and coffee for me and a Coke for Jackie. She felt a new woman, bless her, for she hated long car journeys, and though she was never sick these days it was never far from her, and she felt miserable, and had cried bitterly before we left at the prospect of such a trip before her.

Then Matthew and Peter went off for meal too, no doubt also to be revived by a Coke. How the kids love that drink!

Peter and Jackie soon slept too, nodding unconsciously, propped up in their seats. It was so uncomfortable that I snuggled a blanket round me and crept onto the floor, to complete oblivion for a couple of hours. Matthew found one single spare seat somewhere on the boat where he too nodded off, rather gladly I imagine.

The next thing we all heard were those rasping French words requesting us to rejoin our vehicles, prior to leaving the boat. Sleepily we obeyed, at about 3.00 a.m. we were on French soil, driving on the right not left, and wondering how it is that French roads seem so much straighter than ours at home. But soon we were all asleep again, oblivious of the passing hours, while Matthew drove us onward towards Brittany.

At seven o'clock the car stopped, and we awoke to find the most beautiful morning – a French morning. Matthew had pulled off the main road to rest for an hour, and unknowingly had parked on a working French farm. Madame was up and gathering in the cows from the fields; the hens wandered around underfoot, to be soon joined by three enormous cocks who were released for their day's freedom.

The air was filled with the scent of summer. The bird sang, and grasshoppers hissed in the grass. Everywhere was peace and sunshine that morning. The flowers were bright in the hedgerows, and among the bramble flowers the first blackberries were setting.

We bought milk warm from the cows, and eggs straight from the hens, from Madame, and saw the rabbits, chickens and geese fed and the cows milked. The children found eggs laid in odd places to their delight, two laid in a space in a haystack, and one enormous one – I suppose it was a goose's egg – tucked in a corner.

It was fun talking to Madame *et* Monsieur, *et la* Grandmère, and to try out our French again. It was good to be alive. The crops and animals all looked so full of health, and the air was like dry white wine that fine morning in July.

We journeyed on, and arrived at our destination at midday. St. Cast in North Brittany.

What a pretty place! It was a small town built of a sand coloured stone with flowers tucked everywhere, especially rich pink and red geraniums and roses.

We found the agency and our apartment, which was excellent and all the English Agency had promised us.

But one thing we had not fully grasped. It said on the brochure that a maid was included in the price. The maid in fact was a delightful French Madame who kept the apartment spotless, washed our clothes and cooked a superb evening meal each day, converting our simple ingredients into a feast fit for a gastronome.

The apartment we set with a large garden round it, huge clusters of white daisies, and to one side a grass and clover field in which cows grazed contentedly. To the other side a cornfield lay before the green headland, beyond which we could see the sea.

It was all we could have wanted, five beds – and chairs, tables and showers in the typical French manner, which meant no easy chairs and no bath. But these lovely French windows which open inwards and completely, to be shut at night with shutters to complete the cosiness.

It's hard to have a great playtime interrupted for a snap!

We knew that this apartment had only five beds, but we were assured that there was room for two more. It was a cancellation at a much reduced rate, and we had taken two camp beds and the bedding to go with them. Otherwise everything else we needed was there.

Our idea of getting a cancellation apartment nearly did not come off, for when we got the list from the agency for July for Northern France, there was not a single flat or villa available. But once again we were blessed and another agency was recommended to us, who had had one that morning, which we took without hesitation.

The town of St. Cast was in North Brittany and set in sheltered north-facing bay. It had several separate beaches which were quite distinct in character. The nearest beach took us walking over the headland down narrow bramble paths and finally down steep concrete steps, until suddenly we came upon La Plage de la Pissotte, a secluded, small and beautiful beach. The smooth silvery sands were dotted about with grey rocks and rock pools, with shallow rock faces along the cliff edge for the children to climb. The peace of this small inlet took our breath away. It was so perfect – and so safe for paddling and swimming, and for our little inflatable plastic boat to Peter and Jackie's delight.

We had long talks about swimming and buoyancy and how puppies dog-paddle in the water, and Peter, who was a real water-baby but couldn't swim at all, started to dog-paddle, and for the first time ever remained afloat. He had started to swim!

The sun poured down on us, and continued to do so each day, softened by the gentle sea-mist which seemed to linger on and off through the day, and settle like a soft quilt over everything at night. It was a good thing for us with our tender town skins! We methodically applied sun lotion, sun hats, tee shirts and long trousers to allow the tan to build up without burning, and only Peter's nose and Matthew's feet looked sorry sights, red and peeling – while the rest of us browned, oh so lightly, bit by bit.

"I'm so lucky," said Jeremy one morning, "God has made me a burn-proof boy, you know," as he saw us fussing about with our tender patches. He was so bronzed and lovely.

La Grande Plage was beautiful too. It was the main beach, and lay with an expanse of silver sands in myriads of sailing boats moored out to see. The sea was blue here like one sees on the picture postcards, and quite clear, with soft dry sand to wallow in, or hard sand for games.

There is a favourite French game called "Balle" I believe, rather like a sand version of our "Bowls" which everyone played and we too – children and adults playing on equal terms. A tiny jack is thrown and then each player has two balls which have to be thrown as near to the jack as possible, the winner being the nearest.

This beach had on it the beach Clubs which seem to be such a very happy French idea, and the *sauvetage* boat – the fast little rescue boat which seemed also to be typical of all the main French beaches during the peak part of each day. Little rubber boats with engines and oars, which ply up and down among the swimmers and boats on the lookout for disasters.

As I sat watching the many little tiny French tots in their bright costumes on the silvery sand, or paddling in the warm sea, their "Maman " or "Papa" standing by, it made me think again about those little ones like Jeremy who had never had a seaside holiday with a Mummy and Daddy that was theirs.

There was still Stuart and Nicola, Pippa and Sarah from Jeremy's nursery, and now baby Christopher that I knew of. My heart still yearned desperately for these children, Stuart especially, who was the first baby I spoke to at the nursery, and who was now three and a half. All these little boys and girls were still waiting for adoption – for a Mummy to come and fetch *them*.

We noticed how soft the French seem to be with their children, and how quiet and happy the children are. And so full of health at this seaside place.

The clubs on the beaches were for children and adults to join, with gymnastics, swings, trapezes, rings, ropes, trampolines, balancing bars and beach games organised for each age of child or for the adults. The clear water attracted the children, and each afternoon the water's edge was a gay sight with the little brown bodies gambolling in the breaking waves.

Jeremy was terrified of the water, and how I felt the lost years of his early childhood, those years of babyhood when we would have played those paddling games with him before he became afraid; but Matthew was marvellous with him, and after one week at the seaside, he was not quite so scared.

Later, we found La Plage de Gallot, another beach in a large rock-edged bay with the yacht club in the distance. This beach had some warm, soft sand hills bounding the landward side, in which we gambolled and rolled endlessly. A diving board was built in the sand, and as the tide came in and surrounded it, it was a place to swim to and jump off. There was also a stream of water flowing across the sands which made a good place for the boys to build dams.

Jeremy stayed so well this holiday, so very different from last year's nightmare, when we had rented a cottage on my friend's farm in Devon, and he slept on an old mattress on the floor. The cottage was old and dusty, and he wheezed, coughed and ailed the whole holiday, and we didn't know why.

Now we'd had the specialist's help. He had told us how to deal with holidays for Jeremy, being intensely allergic to house dust, dust mites and feathers, we were able to cover the mattress and pillow with plastic and Sellotape them in completely. We did not actually do that but we took a camp bed with us, clean blankets and a change of sheets. We shook the canvas and bedding outside each day and the apartment was kept clean and dust free. Jeremy had no pillow, and with his spinhaler each day and an anti-allergy medicine each night, he remained in perfect health, robust and smiling.

One wonderful thing that happened one evening at the apartment. Eight magnificent-looking cows had been brought into the field next to our house that morning, and at about six o'clock we saw a sight that is rare for us to see nowadays. Two pretty milkmaids came into the field and sat down on tiny stools and milked the cows by hand, while the cows stood completely still, and quite relaxed, a wisp of their tails tied round a back leg to stop it swinging, the white milk splashing with that particular splash of hand milking into the pail beneath. It looked so fresh and rich and frothy as it was poured into the churn, and the cows continued their day as ever, contentedly chewing their cud, or wrapping long tongues round the stalks of grass, watched for a long time by five young faces.

The French seemed to play so many ball games on the beach, but never once did I see them playing our special game – changing underneath towels. One of us always seemed to be contorted, trying feverishly to maintain our privacy, while dragging off a sandy wet costume or replacing it with normal English underwear. Never did I ever see a single French family all wearing jerseys after swimming as we did during the cooler sunless patches. How very British we must have looked, especially with our tartan rug spread out on the sand!

The highlight of the holiday for me was the night that Matthew took me out for dinner. We went to an attractive hotel on the sea front, called of course, Hotel Belle Vue and were determined to take in as much of France as possible. Our French was really almost non-existent, but we were determined to keep our end up.

"Bonjour, Monsieur, Madame."

"Une table pour deux, s'il vous plait," said Matthew.

This was followed by a tirade of fast French from the head waiter.

"Non," replied Matthew smilingly.

We were taken to a table by the window and sat down. "How cleverly I understood when he asked if we had booked a table," said Matthew.

"But he didn't ask you that," I replied, "He asked if you were a resident at the hotel." It would have been exactly the same if he had asked Matthew if her were the President of the Rebublique – he really hadn't understood a word. If the head waiter had said "Avez-vous booke une table?" then that would have been easier, but not really French French!

Clearly we would have to make the most of talking while we had a waiter in attendance. "What are the curtains called?" I asked in French.

"Oh, they are just curtains," he replied, still in French.

I only wanted to know which word was curtains and which was flags in French. They had just brought an English flag to the table, and I was confused. Drapeaux – flags. Rideaux – curtains. It would never do to thank them for their curtains at such a moment.

Only just before we left the apartment that night I had said (in my best French) to Madame who was baby-sitting for us that especially for her I was going to comb the horses that evening. Of course, I meant to say that I would comb the children's hair. But I do notice a queer expression come over the French when we start talking to them. I don't think they understand French too well!

"Is it alright to say 'le milieu de la table'?" asked Matthew. "Et le milieu de la salle'?" A breath of French from the past had floundered to his consciousness.

"Yes, you can say 'le milieu de' whatever you like," replied the waiter charmingly in his excellent English.

I had the feeling he thought Matthew was soon going to ask for the lavatory.

No vegetables were served with the meal, surprisingly, and so Matthew asked, on my behalf, if I could have the watercress that was decorating the steak. Do all English ask to eat the decorations? I felt them eying the small vase of flowers on the table in case they went next.

We found that in that smart hotel at 8.30 in the evening, there were too many children of all ages eating dinner in the dining room. The atmosphere was so relaxed. People were dressed informally, and many men wore open necked shirts, no jackets, and conversation flourished between the tables. But the service was quite remarkable in that it was impeccable, as well as the meal, which had included cockles cooked with butter, parsley and breadcrumbs. I did something I never in my life thought I could do. I ate them. Until Matthew jokingly said that one was alive. I screamed and dropped it, and couldn't feel quite the same enthusiasm to go on with such a delicacy after that.

In fact, the French do eat them raw, as well as cooked, and later we were shown how to find them ourselves on the beach. In the wet parts of the sand, the cockles lie buried about one or two inches under the surface. To locate them, one had to press the sand with one's foot and watch for where there was a cockle a tiny spurt of water would come up, sometimes an inch or so high, but occasionally a foot high. The higher the fountain, the bigger the cockle! That night after much searching, en famille, we came back with 62 cockles, quite a feat, if you like that sort of thing!

They call all those sort of shell fish – cockles, mussels and oysters "fruits de mer" – fruits of the sea. What a marvellous way to describe nature's marine bounty.

On one Sunday of our holiday, a fete was held at the port, a most informal and pleasurable affair. There were speed swimming races, sculling and rowing races for the boats, a tug of war between rowing boats and races to catch a duck. The duck was taken a few hundred yards out to sea in a motor boat, while all the swimmers lined up at the water's edge. The flag was lowered for off, and the duck was put into the water, to be fast approached by about twenty splashing, thrashing swimmers – one of whom was Matthew each time. The duck took no notice of the pandemonium until they were very close, when he flapped his wings and flew out of everyone's reach. This happened several times until finally, and triumphantly, he was caught and brought back to land.

In the later races I think he knew he had to get caught for he started to swim for he started to swim towards the splashing bodies, making a very easy catch. But still Matthew didn't succeed! With the competition of all the young men and strong boys, he felt it sensational that he once actually touched the duck!

The children have all picked up a little French, and I notice that quite unconsciously Rosemary does a tiny bob-curtsey like the French girls, when she shakes hands and says "Bonjour Madame" to someone. Louise has learnt one word by heart – la plage, which means the beach and every now and then a voice can be heard practising it. I fancy that if anyone asked her anything in French, she would simply reply, very confidently, 'la plage'. She was playing the language game very well indeed!

We often noticed groups of children walking rather quietly round the town, or playing together on the beach, and thought them to be an orphanage on holiday, or perhaps situated here. But we found them to be "les colonies des vacances", a French holiday camp system, which operates all over France, bringing the town children for a month's holiday by the sea. The group I spoke to were all children of "Electricite de France" employees from Paris. The cost to the parents was £3 for each child for the month, the balance being paid by the Electricity Company. In this camp, one hundred children were in a house kept especially for these holidays, and were all between six and nine years old. Girls were looked after by girl students, who were paid £25 per month to care for the nine children in their group, and young men looked after the boys, each one also to a group of nine children. Each camp had, in addition, a director, his wife, a nurse, a cook and a housekeeper in charge of overall management, I was told.

What an interesting concept this is. I could not imagine such a thing on a large scale in England, but the continuously better weather makes a great deal of difference, and also the patrolled beaches with the first aid cabins. I had the feeling too that here the children are more disciplined in a softer, tender way, and loved more openly than perhaps we do in England.

Towards the end of the holiday, we managed to join all five children into the Club for one day, and what a happy day it was for them. The Club's mottos "Be strong to be useful" and "Health though joy" seemed most appropriate to these happy children. Much care was used in bringing every child into play and successful gymnastics, the young and not very good, and the very accomplished young men who were taken further with their skills.

I made fresh peach ice cream during those restful days, no doubt spurred on by the delicious French ice cream sold in little road side kiosks. There was lemon, strawberry, nut, vanilla and blackcurrant, all mouth-wateringly delicious, if a little expensive.

The peach ice cream was made with seven ripe peaches, which I peeled and stoned, and then mashed as finely as possible with a fork. To this I added two tablespoons of sugar and half a pint of double cream and stirred it all well. Then it went into the freezer on a cold setting, to be stirred once or twice very thoroughly before I used it. It made enough for seven voracious appetites or twelve normal size helpings, and was a most delectable ice cream, throughout which were tiny lumps of fresh peach. The best yet, Matthew thought!

I slept with Jackie one night and we talked a little in the privacy together as we fell asleep.

"Is Jeremy really ours now?" she asked.

"No, not really," I replied. "We still have to wait for legal adoption."

"What does that mean?" she asked.

I explained what it meant.

"Could his mother ask for him back now?" she asked.

"Yes, she could, but it is not very likely."

"That would be awful, for even I feel that he is one of our children now," said Jackie with feeling.

"Yes, so do I," I replied.

"What would you do if she did want him back?" asked Jackie.

"I'd try to bring her into the family the first time without telling Jeremy," I said, "so that she could see him, then I'd try to handle as much as I could myself – to make him feel that it was a wonderful thing that had happened."

Jackie went on with her thoughts. "He was so behind when he came to us, and he has caught up with ordinary children now. I think if he had been in the nursery much longer he would have been too behind ever to catch up."

"Do you find him a completely normal little boy now?" I questioned.

"Yes, I do," said Jackie.

"I do too," I replied, as we fell into the last sleep of our holiday, "but don't mention to Jeremy what we have been talking about. He is too young, and is so settled and happy, and it's not very likely to happen."

The holiday fortnight wound gently to an end. We looked like contented zebras, with white stripes under bikinis and costumes, and all the rest of our bodies richly bronzed. We all took our last bath in the French shower – wallowing like Buddhas sitting in the shower our fat tummies bulging between our bent knees as we relaxed against the corner wall.

"Mummy, what do you say when you want to say 'Merci' in English?" asked Louise, as we packed up. She had forgotten what it was!

We journeyed back on a Norwegian boat from Cherbourg, and Matthew had allocated that we would eat on the boat, in the hope that with full tummies we might have a peaceful six hour journey through the night back to our home.

The dinner was a great success. We ate in the Smorgasbord

restaurant, and to everyone's delight, we were all told to eat what we liked and as much as we liked, choosing the food from the colourful selection of cold foods and salads from the centre table.

Louise went up with an empty plate, selected one single slice of orange decorating a salad, and settled back in her place joyfully, to eat her feast! She did return later to replenish her platter, and fill up with huge platefuls of jelly and trifle, and a Coke, of course!

Everyone had mountains of just what they fancied. I had a sea-sickness pill, and just managed to maintain my equilibrium! Matthew had a plateful to sustain him through the night, and along with the other millions moving to and fro that night, it seemed that we were soon home and in our own beds.

It was wonderful to be home. The holiday had been sensational, and worth every bit of saving up for.

Towards Legal Adoption

1

The first official forms arrived, with a warm business letter from Head Office to say that the adoption procedure was commencing, as required, by the Adoption Act of 1958. Two forms were to be signed by us: one returned to Head Office, and one to be sent to the Children's Officer of the Local Authority Children's Officer of the Local Authority Children's Department, notifying them of our intention to adopt a child. I would have left this until after the chaos of the school holidays had subsided but before this was sent off by me however, a Local Authority Child Care Officer arrived exactly in the middle of Louise's fourth birthday tea.

Ten children were seated round the table; five of them under four years old and a little apprehensive about being without their mothers.

"Good afternoon," she introduced herself. "I am the Child Care Officer from the Children's Department.

"Good afternoon," I replied, shaking hands. "This is a terrible moment for you to call. We are in the middle of a children's party. I can't really talk to you at the moment."

"I have been here twice before already to find you out, and we are very busy you know. I must see you this time," she answered. (It was the end of July and we had been on holiday)

"Please do not say who you are," I requested, as we walked into the house through the back door – the front door was locked and the key mislaid!

My Mother, a German guest and my sister-in-law were in the kitchen with the children. It would have been a disaster to announce the nature of the visit at such a time. My Mother had accepted Jeremy himself wonderfully, but would never accept the concept that with four beautiful children, it was good to adopt another. The German lady knew not that Jeremy was other than our own, and had never asked, and I think my sister-in-law found our family large and cumbersome, with only one beautiful child of her own.

We entered the kitchen – the joyful birthday atmosphere disappeared with the appearance of a stranger. I introduced the lady by name. There was no warm smile by my Mother or the children, and no cheerful enquiries about the birthday girl. Nothing. I carefully went round the children and introduced each one by name, to give the Child Care Officer an opportunity to observe Jeremy before he was aware of being watched. But it was absolutely lost, for she did not know the name of the child, and did not recognise the boy who was the reason for her mission.

We stood. I continued looking after the children. None of the other grown-ups were really suitable to take over from me, as I was the only person whom the younger children knew. The Child Care Officer just stood, and I realised that she was not going to go and come back later.

"Could you please hold the fort?" I asked my Mother. "I will just take this lady into the lounge for a minute."

We walked through. She sat down and took out a questionnaire and started to write it pressing on my rosewood writing desk. I slid a magazine under her paper to save the veneer.

We started on the questions. I could feel the tension rising.

"What is your husband's job?" she asked.

"What does that matter?" I replied. "Does it really matter if he is a bus driver or a teacher, in business or a lawyer?"

She assured me that they all knew about people, and this wasn't a kitten they were placing, but an infant.

"But he's a boy, not a baby," I said, "and he had been with us for two years."

"But we do like to place a bus driver's child with a bus driver family."

I felt I couldn't go on, and told her what Matthew's job was.

"What's his business address? What is his income?" came the next two questions.

I wasn't prepared to tell her this. "This is Matthew's private business," I said, "and neither are relevant to us adopting a child." Did it matter if we were earning £1,000, £2,000, or £3, 000 per year?

The veiled threat appeared. "I have to make my report and state that you refused this information on my visit, and this may make a difference at the Court. The judge will certainly want this information.

"What is your job?" I didn't answer. "Housewife," she replied to me. I didn't inform her that I was a writer, and a general dogsbody too. "Have you a private income?" This, I thought, was the end of impertinence.

"No, I haven't." I replied angrily. Was I supposed to tell her that I sold pots of homemade jam to my friends?

And so it went on. "Does the child have a room of its own?" she asked.

Hell, I thought, how many children do have a room of their own. Does it matter? Isn't it better to share a bedroom than live your whole life in an orphanage? "Actually, he does happen to have a room of his own," I said. "I shall have to see that."

Thank God having a natural child isn't like this. Will she inspect his head for dandruff, I wondered. I was ill at ease and showing it. I regretted this further intrusion into the sanctuary of our family life.

"Has he been vaccinated and immunised?"

"As a matter of fact, he has, but it is a voluntary thing, and what has that got to do with adoption. Many people feel that there are grave ill effects from immunisation and vaccination and don't feel it a right thing to do. So many babies die each year from vaccination," I replied.

"But our judge is very keen on this and is most knowledgeable," she replied.

"Oh, that's nonsense! Immunology is a specialised subject, so wide and deep that I doubt that a judge would know much about it at all." I actually knew of three doctors who felt the risks to be so great that none of their ten children had been immunised or vaccinated. I had one friend whose child was unconscious for nine hours following vaccination. My sister-in-law thought that her son was going to die during a brief crisis lasting just thirty minutes after he had been done.

Yearly at present, the number of deaths of children following vaccination is greater than the deaths from smallpox in Britain.

I wished the interview were over now, for the tea party had long finished. The children and adults kept coming into the lounge and I had to send them out in order to talk privately. It was a party and this was most embarrassing.

"Have any payments been made for the child during the two years?" she asked.

"Yes." I told her the amount.

"But I'll find out all the details of that," she replied. Finally, she went.

A grown-up came into the room again. "What did she want?" she asked.

"She came on business," was all I replied.

"It frightens me to do business with someone like that," she answered.

I just wished that I was one of those sweet 'yes women' who said yes all the time and submitted graciously. But then we would not have had Jeremy. I was going to hate this further prying into our family life. There were to be more medicals for Matthew and me and Jeremy, for the third time.

Supposing we found that Matthew was going to die in a couple of years, it would make no difference to me. The kids and I would all stick together. Supposing we had our medicals, then soon after Matthew had a bad car accident and became a paraplegic. I had already got early osteo-arthritis in my knees and hips. Matthew had apondylolithesis. Jeremy was allergic. But no doctor would discover these at a medical unless we told him, or unless he read through every word on our National Health Service notes.Supposing we filled in the forms and declared Matthew's income – next week he could be redundant and jobless.

It all suddenly seemed so ridiculous. We were prepared to share our whole life with this person – could he not take his chance with us, or were we finally to be told that we were inadequate to adopt him.

Quite simply – we were told – if we did not fill in every detail asked for on that form, there could be no adoption. No longer was it a question of a happy developing child, surrounded by people prepared to be loyal through difficulties, but a form that had to be filled in completely, or no adoption could take place.

Our reference had to be seen once again and this worried me, for I knew her to be getting old, having great difficulties and very overworked already. She had filled in forms and been interviewed very fully nearly two years ago, and now it had all to be done again.

But I handed the Child Care Officer the form notifying the Local Authority of our intention to adopt Jeremy, and so we started the three months probationary period. Jeremy's natural mother had to be seen again and sign the adoption form and also his father, although six years had elapsed since he was refused the right to love and care for the girl who was the mother of his child.

How could they feel to have their past all dug up again? Had they committed a crime? They had loved each other, but by now they must surely have made new lives for themselves?

2

However, here we were at home from holiday and back at work again! For two weeks we had drunk fresh milk, warm from the healthiest-looking cows I've ever seen, real, living milk, and bathed daily in the warm sun, and eaten nothing but fresh local grown food. Now we all felt relaxed and soft, and as Matthew said beaming from ear to ear, it was easier to smile again! He came home from business so early in the evenings for a while after we returned, and he said that he was whisking effortlessly though his work, he felt so fresh!

Now we had to think of what to eat the English way again.

Two ideas we had brought home with us gave added pleasure to the children's meals. One was potato puree, instead of mashed potato. The boiled potatoes were either pushed through a sieve, liquidised in the liquidiser or passed through a mouli, after which salt, pepper, butter and milk were added until a fairly thick puree was formed, which everyone found delicious, and, of course, very smooth.

The other idea was not really new, but new to me. Just tomatoes, skinned by immersion in boiling water, and cut up and poached in butter with salt and pepper. Tomatoes were only one and sixpence per pound on our return holiday, and cooked like this, they made a tasty vegetable served with fish.

Peter had another idea for cooking from "Blue Peter" on television, and quite on his own made some chocolate and rice-crispy covered apples.

He took eating apples, plain chocolate, Rice Krispies and wooden meat skewers, and washed and dried the apples and stuck one meat skewer firmly into the centre of each. The chocolate was broken up and melted in a bowl, placed over a pan of boiling water, until it was soft and runny. The apples were then dipped into the melted chocolate, until they were completely coated, and then dipped into a bowl of Rice Krispies until they were covered all over, and left to cool.

They were absolutely scrumptious – and terribly expensive!

I had another crunch biscuit recipe which we used a lot in the family – again very easy and economical:

1 1b. margarine or butter
4 teaspoons syrup
8 do. lemon juice
2 do. (rounded) Bicarbonate of Soda
4 cups of sugar
4 cups S.R. flour
4 cups oats

Melt margarine, syrup, bicarb., sugar and lemon juice in a saucepan over a low heat. When cool, add flour and oats. Roll into small balls and place on greased trays. Cook at Gas No. 3 until done, approximately 10 minutes.

I had also been trying Chocolate Ice Cream with success again. It seems that ice cream is everybody's favourite all the year round:

The children have all got voracious appetites and of course they are getting older all the time, and hungrier, and sometimes feeding them is quite a task! We eat a pound of homemade jam in one meal and a new pot of honey lasts two teas! I have to make about eighty pounds of jam and marmalade to last us through the year and bottle sixty bottles of fruit, or as many as possible, to last us through the winter, filled with rhubarb, apples or blackberries or with whole boxes of fruit picked up at a good price from the market.

Jeremy eats enormously for a small boy of five, often as much as Daddy, and has a reputation for being greedy. In fact, he just eats very well, and sometimes it gets shoved in a mite too fast! He is tall and slim for his age, and I fancy rather handsome, if I may say so.

Christel, the German girl staying with us, had some wonderful English. She told me, so seriously and wide-eyed, that she had an electrician in her frock, and later that she had found a boy in a coffee. What next, we wondered!

Our friends, Diana and Richard have just bought an old car, to Diana's delight and Richard's terror – for he knows not about old cars. Their enthusiasm prompted them to take off a wheel to see if they could improve the brakes. They followed the instruction manual to the letter and all went well until the time came to put the wheel back, for it was then that they discovered they had placed the jack on the warm tarmac, and, gradually, unnoticed by them both, the jack had sunk slowly into the soft surface – just too far to get the wheel back on.

Diana's little boy of two and a half is a real little buster, full of character and sweetness – and mischief. Three times on one day he went right away from his home to play, to be well-thrashed and put to bed each time he was found. As Diana put him to bed that night, he put his arms round her neck – and said so softly, "Sorry about all the trouble, Mum." And all of two and a half years old!

The children's Speech Day at school was a pleasant affair and Jackie was in a lovely show called 'Little Gypsy Gay', which was put on by the children. It was a story about gypsies who found a baby and brought her up, a fair haired blue-eyed girl, in a band of swarthy gypsies. She often wondered why she felt a longing for certain things – a roof over her head instead of the stars, fine sheets to lie between and beautiful clothes, and on her tenth birthday the gypsies told her how they had found her and how much they loved her. She was given the pearl necklace that she had been wearing when she was found.

Her real parents happened to pass by and they told the gypsies of their sad tragedy which had blighted their life ten years ago. They were shown the pearls which they recognised, and a happy reunion followed. Little Gypsy Gay returned home joyfully, with the promise that each year on her birthday, she would spend the whole day with the gypsies, so that they would not miss her too much. It was the gayest of musicals – full of colour and naturalness, dancing and singing, and with a cast of about fifty children.

Jackie had won the needlework prize for really beautiful work. Peter had won a certificate for elocution – (reciting the most gorgeous rhymes most expressively!) His favourite was one which caught all our imaginations, with water rat assuming a dark and gruff personality!

"Ten little tadpoles swimming in a pool,
'Come' said the water rat, 'Come along to school'
'Come and say your tables, sitting in a row'
And all the little tadpoles said, 'No, No, No!'
Ten little tadpoles swimming in and out,
Jumping and diving and turning all about.
'Come' said their mother, 'it's dinner time I guess'
And all the little tadpoles said, 'Yes, Yes, Yes.'"

At the end of it all came the school song, sung softly by the children, and accompanied on the piano.

"|Take the life, that God has lent,
Teach me now its true intent,
Show me how to make the best
Of the gifts which in me rest.
Lead me so that I may win,
Rise victorious over sin;
Bring to me Thy selfless zeal,
Purpose in my life reveal.
Teach me how to offer up
Earthly failures bitter cup,
Show me how to use success
In the way that God will bless.
When my childhood days are done,

Guide me on till life is run,
Then through victory shall I rise
To accept the heavenly prize."

3

The Voluntary Society Child Care Officer called and told me a true story that really warmed the heart. She had a family who wanted to adopt a new-born Anglo-Indian baby girl, but as these were rather rare, she felt she could not promise them one; perhaps older babies from the nurseries, but not a newly-born one. So all one morning she tried to telephone London to ask if they could give her a baby, but failed to get through.

Finally, in the afternoon, she tried again and succeeded. To her amazement, they had such a baby, which had been accepted by the society from a Local Authority only twenty minutes earlier.

If she had been able to make the telephone call that morning, the answer would certainly have been "No" but now it was "Yes" and the family got their baby, and the baby got a home. Miracles really do happen, if only one can perceive them.

We were reminded of a story we were told about another couple who were trying to adopt their first baby. They were also an older couple and the Child Care Officer was a young, long blonde-haired, unmarried graduate, almost half their age, straight from college. After a little talking, she asked the husband if the couple's sex life was normal.

With an admirable presence of mind, he looked straight into the girl's eyes and said, "I don't know what normal is – would you please be kind enough to tell me?"

The 'Notice of Intention to Adopt' was returned to us later by post, as it required another signature and dating more fully, and once again, the accompanying letter was signed with a name that did not,

I thought, belong to the writer of the letter.

I did wish that, as in other walks of life, the letters could be signed by the writer. Surely it is quite wrong if one thinks one is dealing with the Children's Officer called Mr. X, to find that in fact Mr. X knows nothing whatever about your case, and that one is dealing entirely with the Child Care Officer Miss Y, who is the writer of the letter. Why is this deception necessary? It seems that signing another person's name is common practice, a strange and bad practice indeed.

Susan was another much loved friend, with a heart of gold, and Louise's Godmother. She was tremendously interested in helping children in care, and, some time ago she contacted the Council and offered to befriend a child, and become an 'Auntie and Uncle' to a boy in a council home. Even for this she had to undergo quite a lot of inspection and tell me much about their private lives, and endured some quite hurtful remarks made in the interviews, because she had a very beautiful home. She had two children and a house always full of other people's children, and was a marvellous and natural mother.

The boy the Council put her in touch with was fourteen years old, when she herself was but twenty-three years old – too close in age to be sensible. But it was a wonderful thing, and John, the husband, was so kind also, and together they befriended him well and joyfully, until at the age of fifteen he was sent back to live with his grandparents, in what Susan and John described as tragic poverty, and quite unsuitable for encouraging his aspirations to become an apprentice carpenter.

I later learned from Susan that when his boy went to live with his Grandma at the age of fifteen, at the time he could earn some money, Susan and John were forbidden by the Child Care Officer to have further contact with him and the boy was forbidden to visit them anymore because he was told "the environments were too different from each other." This, in spite of the fact that Susan and John were among the boy's only real friends, and that they were willing to assist him to go to college, which was what he really wanted.

I learned too that although John and Susan had asked to have him for Christmas, and it was they who took him home at Christmas when he left for the Children's Home, he in fact spent Christmas entirely alone. The Child Care Officer had refused them the opportunity to share this happy time with him.

After this, they again offered to befriend any child in care, and a nine year Anglo-West Indian girl was allocated to them. Again they gave her a warm welcome in their family and for a very long time persevered with the friendship. But in spite of liking John very much and being very happy with the children and with the house, she absolutely hated Susan, and nothing Susan could do made any difference, and the intense antagonism continued without improving.

Susan and John, being the sort of people they are, would not just abandon the venture, but got very little help in solving their problem. After much persistence by themselves, they finally got to the bottom of it. Susan had long blonde hair. The child's mother had had long blonde hair and the child was treated with great cruelty before she was removed from her. So it would probably never have been possible to overcome such an obstacle.

How tragic – for there are not many women with long blonde hair and clearly the barrier was just too great to be overcome.

This was an entirely avoidable situation, for this type of information should be on the case history of the child, and a great pity too, for John and Susan had real love and interest which could have been a useful rebuilding factor in a young life.

Susan was one of those people to whom everything crazy in life happens. One morning, while she was noticeably pregnant with the youngest baby, she was driving along to do the shopping, when suddenly she felt faint. She quickly stopped the car at the side of the road, got out of the car, and fainted completely on the pavement right in front of a policeman.

After some time, she came round and he insisted on her taking a breathalyser test, cautioned her for parking on a double yellow line, and then allowed her to drive herself home. All that before eleven o'clock in the morning!

Susan's oldest girl was four and a quarter years old and still wetting at night, while her sister of two and a half was quite dry, so we worked out a schedule for her which, to my delight, worked, and she became dry each night.

The idea was to start a programme with her which she could consciously help, so that she could be successful in keeping dry, and enlist her co-operation to stick to the routine every night until Susan felt sure that one waking could safely be dropped.

> *No drinks after 4.p.m. The last drink to be milk, not fruit juice.*
> *Use the toilet before going to bed (6.30 p.m).*
>
> *Two hours later again wake her and walk her to the toilet to do a 'wee' (8.30 p.m.)*
>
> *Put the alarm clock on for 4.30 a.m. and wake her and walk her to the toilet. Make sure that she does not drink any water in her bath!*

This was the routine I had used with Jeremy and it gives the child a chance to be successful. Jeremy was now completely dry, and never more did I wake him or restrict his drinks. Effortlessly he now woke himself when nature called him to the toilet.

It seems that some children miss the boat in becoming dry at night at around two years old, sometimes for no more reason than that they are not taken out of nappies at that age, or that they learn to sleep too deeply to wake on their own, and then they need some practice help to achieve it later on.

4

How much I longed to take another child, younger than Louise this time, for I still had the love to spare, and room in the house for one more. But now I knew for certain that Matthew could not support another child. As much as I wanted it I knew that this dream could only come true again if I earned enough for one more child, and it had to be enough to allow me to have extra help in the house to do the actual physical work of running the family.

We lived on the edge of a precipice financially, and work wise the house was often not quite as clean as I would like it to be, but I was never able to relax for one moment in the fight to make ends meet from day to day.

I could see no reason why foster parents could not be paid an allowance truly covering the full cost of the foster child. I still see no reason why a family should be expected to subsidise a foster child's care and I consider that without doubt, most foster parents do have to subsidise their foster children's care from their own pocket, or in some way earn the extra money to make up the deficit occurring due to the cost of the child.

Compared to the cost of keeping a child in a Children's Home,one wonders if foster parents are used as cheap labour. Nowhere else is it possible to obtain full board and lodging, clothing, etc. for the amount paid as a fostering allowance for 52 weeks of the year.

One wonders if the fact that foster parents must continuously subsidise the foster children contributes at all to the high breakdown rate of even what could be successful fosterings. I heard of one family who had fostered a girl happily for eight or nine years, the brother being in a local Children's Home, and when Gran became incapacitated and needed the bedroom, the foster child had to go. This is clearly a responsible family and one showing concern, and one wonders if the prospect of supporting two extra people so heavily was simply too much for the husband. Clearly there has to be enough money for foster parents to have a bit of leeway, for quite unexpected expenses can occur as a result of the child. For example, many foster children will be eneuretic and the washing will be far more than normal. Perhaps in this case, an extra bedroom would have had to be built onto the house in order to make room for the foster child and Gran as well. The cost of one year's stay in a Children's Home (now about £4, 000) would have gone a long way towards building an extension onto the house as an extra bedroom.

I compiled an estimate of the extra costs that we incurred in the first two years of Jeremy as a foster child and we had to find this money in cash to make a successful venture (appendix). They are all extra costs to any we would have had if we had not had Jeremy, and extra on top of the cost of his food and clothing, shoes, boots, cleaning and washing, heating, treats, outings and spending money.

It can also be said that because of Jeremy, we'd had to move to a larger house, for with four children who were all tremendously healthy we could just manage in our tiny Sussex bungalow, but with five children all crowded together and one ailing continuously, it was imperative to move before Matthew and all of us went quite, quite mad. If we had been unable to move, our venture might have been liable to fail on that account alone, not for lack of love but simply because of the physical pressure of all being crowded together, and not being able to get any privacy or quietness away from each other.

We had to have enough money to support the move, yet had we not taken Jeremy, the chances were great that he would have spent the rest of his life in a Children's Home, to which he was just due to go when we took him. There is no reason too, why a small allowance should not be paid for doing this work, for surely the overall care of a foster child for 168 hours per week is worth at least as much four mornings of domestic work, or two mornings teaching or one afternoon of dentistry in the school dental service.

There are so many people who I am certain could and would do this work, but they must have a chance to do it under satisfactory circumstances.

5

We have at last found another Godfather for Jeremy, a delightful young man who works with Matthew, and who entertained us so warmly while we were in Sussex. He is a lovely person – a keen Christian, and famous for being absent minded. The story goes that he once came home, kissed his large rumbustious dog, and patted his wife on the head. I don't suppose it was quite true, somehow!

He wrote back, and I thought how pleasing it was to receive a nicely handwritten letter:

> *This is to say a very real thank you for kindly inviting me to be Godfather to Jeremy.*
>
> *I shall be most happy to perform this function and feel it a solemn privilege. No doubt you will let me know when the christening is to take place.*
>
> *It will be good to see you all again as a family. Our affectionate greetings to you all.*
>
> *Phillip*

There was not actually going to be a Christening though, for Jeremy had been baptised at the nursery as a baby, when it looked as though no family were forthcoming for him.

He had been given a little prayer book on that day by the Church where the ceremony was performed, and this he cherished, so much so that it was frequently carried around with him, and having been left in the rain one night, now looks a bit the worse for wear.

"You can borrow this when you go to Church, Mummy, if you

want. I don't really understand about Church yet, but I do understand about God," he said one day.

What an apposite remark from a small boy! How I sympathised!

We had been fortunate here with a vicar who was blessed with the most gorgeous wink, especially reserved for wriggling boys and girls as he walked back down the aisle each service. I am sure this wink would win more men for Christ than all his sermons! Certainly more boys and girls!

The Adoption Society never told us that in fact we were adopting Joe Bloggs, the boat builder, when we took Jeremy. Excited by the holiday trip I suppose, Joe Bloggs and his brother Fred, have emerged, and all day long there is a distant hammering and sawing to be heard in the garage, and profuse quantities of Matthew's beautiful copper nails disappear from the jars.

There are some bits of wood on the pond now. And two boys always up to their elbows in water!

The holiday photographs had come back, and what a joy they were. One little series showed Jeremy with one of the cows in the field behind our apartment, actually milking the cow himself. It was a real success story for with a tug, a pull and a squeeze out came a little trickle of milk from each teat. Not quite the dab hand of the experienced milkmaid, but not bad for a beginner.

He was good with animals; he was gentle with them, and I think they sensed that he liked them a great deal too.

6

I bought a copy of the 1958 Adoption Act and searched avidly through it, noting that the only actual information required was our names, ages, Matthew's occupation, our address and evidence of our health. I had been told that all the information that I had been asked for again by the Children's Department was required by the 1958 Adoption Act.

In section 7 (part lb) it stated "that the (adoption) order if made will be for the welfare of the infant", so I suppose that this gives the Court an open chance to pry and check to any degree they want to.

Nowhere, however, did I find any reference to the fact that the Local Authority Children's Department would go through the whole vetting procedure again, that we had already undergone with the Adoption Society. I later learned that the Judge in this district is a middle-aged bachelor who does not agree with adoption. Not a man who has experienced a vigorous family life in all its richness and abundance, but one who was well known for demanding the completion of every detail on the form before he would grant a court order.

It was made clear to me that if I said anything at all outspoken, it would result in the Judge deferring the granting of a court order. So we had no alternative but to comply meekly. If I expressed any opinion about anything, I would be considered "unsuitable"!

There was an alternative in law, but one which, in our case, would be a difficult and long drawn-out procedure. We could go through the High Court which would allow this particular form to be dispensed with, but it would involve the finding of every person who had ever been involved in the case of Jeremy, the midwife, the mother, the Child Care Officers, the nursery matrons, ourselves and each of these eight people would have to swear an affidavit, in order to prove the identity of the child. Rather a tall order!

It is strange to think that all this particular heartache could have been avoided by the Council waiting until they had received my "notice of intention to adopt" form, and then making a friendly introductory phone call, so that I could have been introduced verbally to the Child Care Officer, and informed a little of the procedure. A few manners oil the wheels of life so well, and never cost a penny. In this case they would have cost sixpence!

I was out into an impossible position in the family with things handled as they were. It would have been so easy for the Child Care Officer to have telephoned and explained that she was the person normally appointed by the Court as the 'guardian ad litem' (Section 9 part 7 of the 1958 Adoption Act) and that it was her job to 'safeguard the interests of the infant before the court'.

When they compile the next Adoption Act, perhaps they could refer to the "infant, child or young person," to eliminate the situation of an older child or teenager coming for adoption and being called an infant continuously as per the Act. Obviously we cannot beat the law, but, at the same time, we must all try to preserve the interests and privacy of the individual, in an age of increasing bureaucratic interference in every aspect of life of every person in our country.

From the cradle to the grave, we are now interfered with. In one house we built some years ago, we were told from which company we had to buy the bricks in order to obtain Local Authority planning permission!

At one primary school, our children were taken to the dentist without me being informed or present, causing great distress to them both.

Sometimes it seems that the Welfare State inflicts such cruelties, and one wishes that it would remember, as a magazine so succinctly put it, that "People are People, are People, are PEOPLE, are P-E-O-P-L-E.

7

There were so many cheap plums about at that time, and I found that the purple egg plums, selling at about 10d. a pound in the local market, made one of the most delicious, easy and inexpensive jams.

3 1bs. purple egg plums
31bs. soft brown sugar

Packet of jam pot covers (1 1b. size)
5 x l1b. jam jars

Method: Wash jam jars and place on a newspaper in a warm oven.

Remove the stalks and wash the fruit well. Put into a large saucepan with a little water and stew thoroughly until the fruit is well broken up.

Add the soft brown sugar, stir well until the sugar has dissolved. (Notice the jam jar at this stage, for it has a beautiful colour and clarity for a few moments.)

Boil fast, removing the stones with a teaspoon as they float to the top, and also any scum that collects at the side of the jam.

Pour a spoonful of jam onto a cold saucer to see if it 'sets' a little. (A slight skin will form which you can see when you push your finger through the jam.)

When it 'sets', pour into the hot jars, cover with waxed discs, wax side down, wipe the jars clean, and cover with the wetted cellophanes held firm with elastic bands, and label.

This recipe makes 5 1bs. of jam at a cost of about 1/6d. per jar. It is super and not lumpy for those fussy children and adults who like a smooth, seedless jam! And it is a pure jam and will keep perfectly for one or two years in a cool place.

Later I found yellow egg plums in the market at 9d. a 1b., and the family thought it also a good jam. Rosemary had helped me make the jam, and not long after she came in crying pathetically, having fallen onto the concrete floor of the garage. She was ashen coloured and wailing and there was a graze on her right temple. She crawled into bed on her own and I watched her carefully while she dozed and wailed restlessly. Two hours later she was no better, in fact worse, and felt ill and very, very sick – signs I knew to show slight brain damage.

I telephoned a doctor, and half an hour later he arrived, by which time she was improving a little. He made a slight examination of her and said that she had just come out of the first phase of a brain injury and should now improve with rest, but that I was to watch for the second phase, which would be difficulty in moving her arms and legs that evening or next morning. After that she should, all being well, be all right.

The headache and nausea passed off thankfully, and she fell asleep, to wake in the early evening when I brought her down to the couch where she could lie with us, but still be quite flat. I explained to her that there was a bruise inside her head and that if she would stay for a couple of days, it would heal up and she would have no headaches later on, and she understood and was a marvellous child, keeping her head for most of the time on the pillow.

That night I tested her plantar reflexes, by stroking the sole of her foot from heel to toe with a pencil, which showed a diminished response on the left foot (the bump was on the right). When I asked her to grip my finger first with the right hand, then the left side, she said it was more difficult to do the left one, although she was normally left handed. There was happily no difference in the strength of her grip.

She slept in the camp bed beside me all night, and was absolutely adorable, and so affectionate, positively overwhelmed with all the extra attention she was receiving. But she slept well and in the morning appeared completely well, no headache, no sickness, and her feet reflexes were exactly the same. She was her pink and radiant self again and her eyes were shining, but just to be on the safe side, I kept her in bed, lying flat, for one more day.

How glad we all were that her bump had healed up so well, with no complications and how thankful we once again felt.

Jackie went up to the greengrocers the other day. "Some potatoes please," she asked.

"How many do you want?" he questioned.

"Two pans full please," replied Jackie.

"What size pans – saucepans?" He was obviously enjoying his sparring partner.

"No, chip pans," said Jackie.

We got our potatoes! Later that same day, another potato customer came in. "The largest potatoes you've got please," she stated. He weighed out his biggest onto the scales. "They are much too big," she scowled!

Obviously it was not his day for potatoes!

Our own home-grown spuds planted last April were at last ready for harvesting, and Peter and Jeremy were my pickers, excitedly gathering a huge bucket full from just two short rows. I kept a tray full for next years seed potatoes and the others were cooked with mint and salt and served with butter to make a real feast, full of flavour. These were an early variety called Arran Pilot.

We have also gathered one solemn marrow, some beans, and two huge bowls of garden spinach which cut up and poached in butter with salt and served with more butter was also scrumptious.

I had obtained a book which I found helpful with my garden called "Fresh Food from Small Gardens" by Brian Furner, published by Stuart and Watkins Ltd. and obtainable from 'The Soil Association', New Bells Farm, Haughley, Stowmarket, Suffolk. It is a book devoted to ordinary folk like myself, trying to grow fresh food for the family in good composted soil, without resorting to the dangerous insecticides and fertilisers with long term side effects of which nobody knows.

There is a way of course, without these chemicals and a proven, better, way, if only one can find out about it, and Brian Furner tells us a little in his book, and encourages us on to further endeavours. He even tells of the Soil Association farm where seven acres have never been dug, never been hoed, no herbicides are used and it is entirely weed free! It sounded unbelievable, but he started me putting a thin layer of grass cuttings over my weeded flower beds, and certainly no more weeds came – that year at any rate!

After a long interval, we were venturing into chickens again. There was a wild part at the end of the garden, and this would provide an abundant supply of fresh green food for a major part of their diet, supplemented by barley, which we hoped was right. They were the most beautiful birds, all at a point-of-lay, and all a rich blue-black and brown, their shiny feathers glinting with an oily splendour, a hybrid variety called Arbor Acres Sex Link. We gave them a large run, wired in around their chicken house, and we were surprised to find that during their first week they ate the run quite barren of fresh food and we had to give them the freedom to scavenge the whole wild patch beyond the lawn.

These already beloved hens laid two dozen eggs in that first week, small brown beginners eggs – (how kind nature is) with just five enormous ones to show what was in store for us.

The hens had been reared organically on a farm specialising in organic husbandry, and had grown up not knowing drugs, hormones, enzymes, insecticides, debeaking or the confinement of a battery house, but had received only fresh air, sunshine, freedom, good food and management, and looked in the most perfect condition when they arrived. They were supplied to us by Springhill Farms (Dinton) Ltd., of Aylesbury, Buckinghamshire.

I had no special knowledge of chicken care at all, and felt very inadequate for the task and started to read every useful manual we could get hold of. But it seemed that most books were now written for

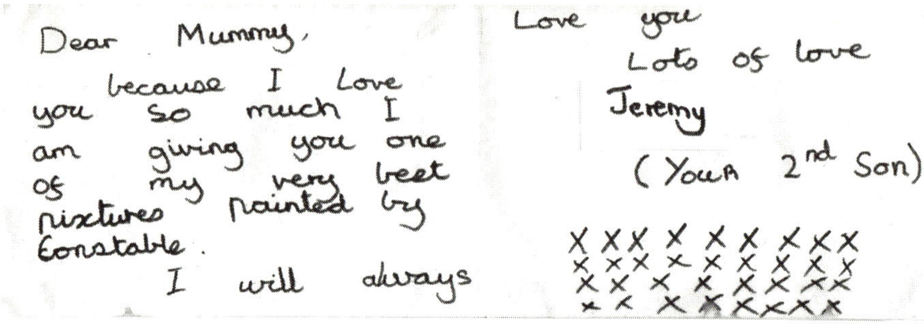
Dear Mummy,
because I Love you so much I am giving you one of my very best pixtures painted by Constable.
I will always Love you
Lots of love
Jeremy
(Your 2nd Son)
XXXXXXXXX
XXXXXXXXX
XXXXXXXXX
XXXXXXXXX

A very treasured letter indeed

my exquisite parsley patch to nibble and scratch it, until it looked so pathetic. My parsley was the very first I had ever grown successfully and it had looked prolific and succulent. I supposed I had better dry some quickly before it was too late and we would have parsley flavoured eggs but no parsley.

The hens gave us so much pleasure, and to our amazement would come and eat from our hands, and some would stand still while we picked them up. Each night they walked back to the hen house, and so we only had to shut their small door at dusk, before the foxes came searching for their supper! And remarkably, we thought, they strode clucking to the hen house each time when the urge to lay an egg overtook them. I was so glad they resisted the temptation just to squat down in the long grass whenever nature called!

The boys were especially delighted with their egg coup, and when they came home from school would race down to the hen house together shouting, "Beat you to get the eggs", to return beaming with one or two eggs apiece, and one some days a triumphant total of four or five.

We made some hay for the laying boxes, shipping the long grass that abounded in the garden and turning it often to dry, and so when it rained, I did not rush out to bring in the washing like other women, but would run out to bring in the hay, and was to be seen staggeringly blindly up the garden looking much like a hay-rick with legs!

8

Louise started school, and after eleven years with little ones around, I was on my own again. I wondered if the town would see two drunken women lurching merrily around as Mavis (whose youngest of five had also just started) and I were simultaneously left off the hook. But no – my Mother took the precaution of inviting me to lunch the first day!

Mavis and I bit our nails together over cups of coffee, through the afternoon, nervously fidgeting the hours away while our bairns gaily sang about Polly getting sick (or was it her dolly?) and had a pink and glowing time, judging by their rosy cheeks and shining eyes. But where were their tensions and tears? It had been hell for us, surely they could not have been so ungracious as to actually enjoy it.

The first day was over. One little girl told the school quite firmly that "Yes, thank you, she loved them all very much but that, thank you, she was not coming any more."

Mavis gave me a book to cheer me up – one that spoke to my innermost being – not my spiritual being, but my domestic one, and it made me very, very happy indeed. Here at last I'd found a friend who knew about my domestic inhibitions and I was not struggling alone.

No longer did I need to feel harassed and frustrated because the aspidistra leaves were not dusted. My untidy, guilt filled rubbish drawers had suddenly been promoted to "clutter depots" – which I now knew were a necessary adjunct to every well balanced family.

No longer did I have to go around pretending to love housework. At last someone had said it for me, and now at last with absolutely best-seller confidence I can almost shout "I hate housework" and smile benevolently. It no longer matters if the ironing pile is mushrooming (so long as there are underpants to wear), if the windows are grubby, our home as at least a place where we can just be us, where we can read The Book in peace, or drink our coffee, or stand with arms akimbo, shouting orders like a demented sergeant-major.

The roof does not leak (I don't think) and with excellent amounts of vitamin A in the diet (there's crunchy carrots for tea) does it really matter an iota if there is no light in the loo, or the hall or the larder or the bedroom. We'll all go to bed anyway if it is too dark.

How wonderful not to pretend anymore, and to be able to snuggle in bed, with only the faintest touch of guilt, and just smile with Peg Bracken the author, and fondle her latest baby "The I Hate to Housekeep Book".

Thank you, Peg.

9

I notice now that Jeremy features less and less in my story, and one might wonder why. He was just one of my family, neither more important nor less important than any other person. Our family life is normal again, uneventful, dull and ordinary – no drama – no emotional crises or hurts any more, and isn't this just what we wanted for Jeremy, not high tension, but just ordinary living in the real world of a family.

The miracle had been achieved. He now has what is a birthright for most people, a mother and father. We set out to give him what he himself lacked, and now that he has it, it does not make news any more. So often in life, it is what one has not got that makes the headlines, and as soon as one has got it, nature allows it to fall into unconsciousness and then one takes it for granted. That is how it should be.

I am sorry that there are not any episodes to tell you now about Jeremy, but rejoice with me over the absence, and be happy that all

I can tell you now are the odd bits of our family life – the framework in which Jeremy will live and grow while we wait for the legal adoption to be accomplished.

But it might so easily have been a different, more remarkable story, of a sad-eyed boy living in a children's home, forever mystified why he had no Mummy and Daddy, sisters and brothers, like all the other boys at school. The very ordinariness of his life now is why we are so very glad.

10

Other older unwanted children have also achieved a normal life in our country through the Children's Family Trust which was set up by Paul Field in 1945, when he took nine boys into his family – for keeps. This total commitment was a new idea in child care – and must surely be the only chance there is of healing the hurts in a child whose own family has irrevocably broken down.

The Children's Family Trust has now established a number of separate Victorian-sized families, taking altogether over one hundred children of all ages. Each family takes the children for always, so that real and long tern security is given to them all, and the children of each family take the surname of their new Mummy and Daddy, so that to the outside world it is a normal relationship. Into these families too, large natural families of scattered brothers and sisters were re-united, never again to be torn apart.

This is a voluntary venture, demanding remarkable people as parents, who will give their whole life to this work, with no turning back, whatever the difficulties, and needing huge amounts of money to establish and finance the families.

The first children have, of course, now grown up, to return to their family homes, year after year with their sweethearts, wives, and their babies and children for family reunions. For family life never really ends, and always there is a Mum and Dad waiting to give them a warm and loving welcome, or Granny and Grandpa to fuss and cuddle their many gorgeous grandchildren.

But what a marvellous work, getting right to the heart of life's problems with a total involvement and total love.

A story that came out of the Children's Family Trust was one of one young boy who had laboriously learned the organ, and was appointed to play at some solemn family occasion. I think it was a wedding. But instead of a sombre wedding march at the appropriate moment, the strains of a jubilant 'Polly Wolly Doodle' echoed through the church, until a somewhat re- faced youngster was persuaded, literally, to change his tune!

Matthew came home again from one of his business sojournings in full strength. "Darling, did you read about the time that Parliament was discussing sewage disposal? Into the sea at coastal resorts", he said. "One desperate M.P. got up to complain about his particular seaside constituency, and bewailed the fact that the situation was so bad that one could no longer swim there but only go through the motions." Only slowly did his faux pas dawn, until apparently, the whole House was completely convulsed in laughter."

Another story to come from the Children's Family Trust was of a baby boy of eighteen months who was accepted by the parents of one of their families, who until that time had never been outside the hospital where he was born, as he was regarded as subnormal and "un-adoptable". Now at five years of age, he is a grand little boy, perfectly normal and a great joy to his parents.

11

It has been suggested that we made some lemon curd, and so we tried some, largely at Jackie's inspiration, as she insisted that for her first school cookery lesson at the new school it must be a lemon curd tart.

The recipe made 2 1bs. of curd, so refreshingly sharp in flavour and a rich saffron colour:

4 lemons
4 free range eggs
1 1b. sugar
¼ 1b. butter

Wash and dry the lemons and grate the rind from each thinly. Then halve the fruit, squeeze out all the juice. Strain the juice into a basin, placed over a saucepan of boiling water, and add the grated rind, beater eggs, sugar and butter. Stir over a gentle heat, with a wooden spoon, until the sugar and butter are melted and the curd thickens to the consistency of thin custard. Pour into hot jars and cover at once.

We were given some rhubarb, the last of the season I suppose, and I served it, just stewed, with some soft brown sugar, adding two pinches of bicarbonate of soda at the end to lesson the sharpness of the fruit.

My domestic help has told me of the way her mother used to make toffee apples for her seven children in the olden days of their childhood. It was simply – 1 1b of treacle, a dessertspoonful of vinegar and a knob of butter all boiled together in a saucepan.

Wooden skewers or sticks are stuck into the well washed apples and then the apples are dipped into the toffee until they are coated and stood on oiled tins to cool.

A likeable feast, with apples cheap at the moment as the new season's crop floods the shops.

I have learnt another thing from her too – that blue-tit boxes must not face south because it is too hot in summer for the babes, or east because of the cold east wind. But facing west or north-west, one will almost certainly have a nest of tiny visitors.

Hilda came round for coffee on Monday and had us both smiling over her love life. She and her husband had been a bit out of sorts with each other for a few days and he had gone to sleep alone in the spare bed.

One morning, he got up and announced that his sheet was torn, and would Hilda please change it that day. But Hilda forgot and that night, rather than incur his wrath, she crept into his bed and lay on top of the tear and fell asleep thinking that he would go into her bed when he came in.

But no, her plan misfired, and when he came home very late and crept into the spare bed (his bed), he felt certain that she was there especially waiting for him because she loved him so.

And that made everything alright again! Hilda was very run down at the time, and I was able to get twenty-five Becosymn Forte tablets for her from the Chemist as a tonic. They are a very good complex of the B vitamins, with no drugs added. I am told, and she took two each day and felt much better after a short while. I have always found this so with these B vitamins, which I had prescribed to me when I was pregnant and breastfeeding my babes, all these years ago, and which Matthew had had recommended by a doctor for eyes that were tired out with driving! So it seems that everyone who needs strength can benefit from them!

12

The Child Care Officer came again from the Council, and as it was exactly at the time I was fetching the children from school, she again found me out.

This system seems not to be very efficient, and one is not surprised that social workers are famous for being overworked and short staffed! We have now had four visits from the Council's Children's

Department, and only one was fruitful – that is 75% inefficiency!

I feared that she would consider us a wildly eccentric family if ever she called to find the hens sitting nonchalantly on the door mat, and I hoped too that she was not scared of hens, for at times they had been known to wander clucking through the house!

She called again another day at the same time and, once more, I was out. That made 80% inefficiency, but the next time, we were actually able to reduce the odds down to 66% of unfruitful visits! She had now tramped to our house six times by bus and on foot for two successful interviews.

What a charming person it was this time. It seemed like another lady, although it was in fact the same one, but now she was smiling and pleasant and spent an hour with us, while the children had tea, and we had a 'cuppa'. This time we were not in an embarrassing situation, no visitors were with us, no questions were asked at all, and she showed commendable tact with the children.

It was important that the children did not know why she visited, for it might bring all sorts of unnatural emotions concerning Jeremy, and in Jeremy at that stage. We had long ago reached the stage of full acceptance of our newcomer; it was all past history in the life of our children and ourselves, and it would be unreasonable to stir it all up now.

She was not afraid of hens! I am glad to say.

I now collected six forms from the County Court, medical forms for Matthew, myself and Jeremy, and two identical application forms which consisted of four foolscap pages, and which it seemed would later inform us of the address of Jeremy's Mother. This form (ACA 1) could have been more clearly written in one respect – the margin notes were not always placed near to the item to which they referred, and so one had to keep jumping from one page to the other to gain explanation of what was meant.

How do less academic folk get on, I wondered, with words like

– undersigned, desirous, provisional, domiciled, ordinarily resident, pursuance, fully registered medical practitioner, deceased, guardian, signifying, documents, dispense, reference, duplicate and confidential – all on the main application form, not counting the margins!

The last form was that for Jeremy's mother and father to sign their consent once again, with a note saying that she would be informed of the day of the Court proceeding and the name of the Court at which it would be held.

This form (ACA 5) required the consent of both of them unless they had abandoned, neglected or persistently ill-treated the infant, or could not be found, or were incapable of giving consent, were unreasonably withholding consent, or had persistently failed without reasonable cause to discharge the obligations of a parent or guardian, in which case it could be dispensed with.

Our identity could be kept from Jeremy's natural parents by the use of a serial number.

The medical forms for Matthew and I required the doctor to sign that we were both "physically mentally and emotionally suitable to adopt a child."

Is there a mother anywhere, I wondered, who feels physically, mentally and emotionally suitable to be a parent!

The medical examinations could cost us another £9.9.0. Why, one wonders, if ante-natal care is given free under the National Health Service, are not adoption medicals included in their services. We had now been without foster-child payment of any sort for Jeremy since 10th July 1969, with no Family Allowances, and no Income Tax allowance, but the Child Care Officer suggested that we should try to get these. I thought ruefully of that glorious maternity grant of £25 which comes as a welcome bonus to launch each natural child into the family – no such good fortune with adoption – only debts imposed by the system, which one tries to avoid if one can.

I would again try to find a doctor who would waive his fees for the medicals, but it would take time and it is embarrassing. One does not ask other professionals to give their services free, and one feels that doctors in the National Health Service are already put upon in so many ways.

What effect too, would yet another medical have on Jeremy, when he knows that other children do not have medicals? How would he feel?

I now learned that alternatively we could go to a Magistrates Court, where the adoption application would be heard sooner. The magistrates sat daily, I was told, whereas the Judge at the County Court sat only once a month for adoptions, and there would be a wait of three more months before the application could be heard at the County Court. I knew almost nothing of Court procedure in England, and I had a deep rooted feeling that the Courts had to do with law breaking and were something to be avoided. But I suppose that one of their main jobs is to try to safeguard the rights of the individual. Some time later I visited the Law Courts and spent a short while sitting in the public gallery to soak in the atmosphere, and try to prepare myself for the visit in some small way.

13

The golden days of Autumn were here again. Late October slipped quietly into November, and still the trees held their russet leaves, and underfoot a bronze carpet crunched merrily as one walked along. The days were sunny and bright, and the children felt happy to play in the clean air, allowed free for a while from the hot classrooms, to romp till bedtime, and school so soon the next morning.

After one earlier attack of bronchitis when the term started, Jeremy was fit and free of coughs, so when a friend asked if he could stay away for the night, I, of course, said yes. He was delighted, for it is always an adventure to stay with a friend.

So with "my" little case packed with his belongings he departed smiling from school to stay with Stuart and his family of three sisters, and obviously enjoyed it all immensely. But on his return twenty-four hours later, he was gasping for breath, wheezing like a trouper, and with that curious expression that I have learned to recognise when he is getting ill.

I popped him into bed, hoping that he would throw it off quickly, but I was terribly disappointed. He had obviously had such a lovely time, and together he and his friend had turned out the toy cupboard, stripped the beds, and no doubt played heartily on the bedroom carpets, and the dust had simply knocked him overboard. He was really ill only a few hours after being so completely well, wheezing, coughing and choked up with mucus.

Now the procedure was to keep him in bed with a penicillin antibiotic and lots of hot, fresh fruit drinks, plus a bowl to cough into, while the allergic bronchitis settled down again.

I had popped him into bed and made him comfortable and Matthew sat down by the gas fire for a cup of tea. Louise came in and started to slam the glass door of the dining room at Rosemary on the other side. Matthew put a stop to that dangerous game and turned his eyes back to his book and his cup of tea. Louise pushed again at Rosemary, pressing hard on the glass, the door clicked shut, and Louise shot right through the glass door, shattering it into a million pieces. She screamed and blood gushed everywhere. I ran to her and saw yawning flesh on one forearm, and clasped my hands tightly around her tiny limb on each side of the wound, to stem the flow of blood from the heart through the severed vessels.

"Quick, quick, Matthew, get her to the hospital."

He rushed out to the car, and I carried her screaming, my hands still tightly pressing on her arm above and below the cut to act as a tourniquet. I never released this, and Matthew roared up the hill and through the town continually flashing his lights and sounding his horn in the way the emergency ambulances do, overtaking wherever safe, and crossing the red traffic lights after checking that all was clear to do so.

Blood was everywhere. My skirt and jersey were saturated, and we sat in a pool of ever increasing blood. But gradually we could see the bleeding was stopping. We knew where the Casualty Department of the Hospital was, and we ran straight in with the child, straight past all the other waiting clients, to the feet of the doctor on duty.

I sat down, with Louise on my knee, and gently relaxed the hold on her arm above the flesh... a glass wound, one of the things I have dreaded and an artery was cut... but miraculously before our eyes, we saw a soft mushy clot forming – nature was doing her bit again. I took my hand right off her slender muscles and we watched carefully, the doctor, Matthew and I. No more bleeding occurred, and the doctor put a thick sterile pad over the wound and bound it firmly with a crepe bandage.

"I'm afraid you will have to take her to the Children's Hospital – we are not allowed to do it here," he said. "I would do it, but it is not permitted."

"But it is Saturday evening, and their Casualty Department is shut?" I enquired.

"I will phone them, there will be someone there," he replied. "There is nothing to worry about."

We drove over to the Children's Hospital in a most leisurely way compared to our urgent journey just those few minutes earlier, and found the Hospital quiet, and not a soul in Casualty. But a light was on in one room and the door ajar, so we put our head round to see a nurse sitting at a table, evidently expecting someone to arrive. "

Are you the cut arm?" she asked. She looked at the wound, and happily no more bleeding had occurred, so she bound it up again, and we waited for the doctor to come back from the wards while Louise slept, and we relaxed.

The doctor came and said that they would now take Louise to clean and suture the wound, but I said that I would come too.

"No, you cannot come," they all said .

"I insist on keeping her company; she would never understand if I suddenly left her now," I replied. In that almost empty department I felt that if they refused to let me stay with her, I would take her elsewhere, and I felt strong enough to stand up to authority.

They yielded, and we went into Casualty Theatre. I popped Louise onto the table and stood beside her, holding her good hand, while the doctor and the two nurses washed their hands and put on masks. Later I got a mask too!

The first thing was to give Louise a local anaesthetic into the skin round the huge gaping wound, so that they could handle it without pain, but it needed about seven injections to go round it all. Poor Louise – she found this awful, and was so brave counting fiercely up to ten as a distraction, but gradually her bravery was gone, and she just screamed and screamed as the tiny needle poured the pain killing fluid into the skin.

Moments later it was done and her arm had "gone to sleep", an idea she found quite acceptable – and true! The doctor lifted up a swab filled, I supposed, with saline, and sloshed the wound with the liquid, and immediately the artery leapt into action again, spurting blood into a huge arc several feet wide, and spattering her white coat and the walls.

"Spencer Wells."

The nurse passed her some artery forceps and she clamped it off, and then ligatured it with a piece of catgut. It did seem a shame to disturb nature's healing clot, but I suppose she had to wash out the wound and check thoroughly for bits of glass. It was all well washed out, and dried, and looked so pale and anaemic at the end!

Suddenly a great dizziness came over me, and I knew I was going to faint. I let go of Louise's hand, and lay quickly on the floor, underneath the operating table on which she lay, assuring them all I'd be alright. I got up telling Louise I had tummy ache, as I thought this a bad moment to try to explain the meaning of faint! But in a moment the world whirled before me again, and I lay down, the cool marble floor strangely friendly to receive me,

I was beaten at the thing I loved best! I had seen many operations before I was married, and only later I remembered that I had been a senior Theatre Nurse for two months, doing my orthopaedics, nearly twenty years ago! But here I was with an important job to do to reassure my child in a strange situation, happily hugging the floor under the table, nonchalantly making small talk to my daughter. Such kindness I've never known. It appeared to the nurse that quite clearly I was determined to stay horizontal, so with considerable aplomb, she wheeled in another trolley, and I crawled onto it, to be next to Louise and once again hold her hand and smile and make small talk to her. How luxurious it was! It was so nice to be fussed! This really was going that extra mile.

Slowly, one by one, ten stitches were inserted, drawing together the edges of the gaping wound and it was dressed with gauze and bandages to an impressive size. Poor girl – two of the most enormous injections came her way then, penicillin into one leg, and anti-tetanus into the other, but it was soon over, and she went home mumbling that she would never push glass doors again, and boasting over her afflictions.

We really were tremendously lucky though, for the artery was not a main one and her hand stayed a good colour and warm throughout the night and next few days showing that the circulation was good, and no nerves were cut. It could have been a terrible accident, but it was all going to be alright, except for a fine, but long and jagged scar.

This bright-eyed picture of Jeremy, after one and a half years with us. He is about 5½ years old and it joins the gallery of portraits that have given a lifetime of pleasure

The Adoption

1

At last another letter came from the Council's Children Department which, once again, appeared to be written by the Children's Officer, signed with his name and which he believed was written by the Child Care Officer dealing with our case. It does seem an unsatisfactory practice, a sort of cloak to work under, which makes passing the buck very easy and divests everyone in the lower realms of real responsibility.

The letter informed us that our Child Care Officer would now have to see us both and complete a form. Oh dear, that would be back again with the two omissions, of Matthew's salary and his business address. I was not looking forward to the meeting!

It was three months since that first meeting at Louise's birthday party and our third visit, but she came and was charming, and as we had arranged if for a time when the children would be in bed, we had peace!

While she went through the form I went discreetly out of the room to make some coffee; my face was far too inclined to blush ruby red and my neck too if I felt worked up or embarrassed, and I wanted not to be there when she got to those crucial questions! The coffee took just the right amount of time to make and when I came back in, we were back on vaccination again! The form was completed.

Matthew later told me he had answered both questions indirectly and she was satisfied with the answers, so everyone was happy.

She recounted one story to us of an older boy in their care who, after years in a Children's Home, was at last boarded out with a foster family. It was winter time and supper was served in front of the fire with Ma and Pa each side of the fireplace and the boy cosily in his dressing gown between them. This obviously was to be the pattern of the evenings in his new home, and on about the sixth night, the boy showed some consternation. He looked from one to the other, a puzzled expression on his brow, "You can't both be on duty again," he said.

The difference between a home and a HOME are enormous.

We asked her again about Family Allowances and Income Tax relief and she said that she thought that Income Tax Relief and Family Allowances are paid to the adoptive parents only after the date that the Court has granted the adoption order.

A few days later, we heard from our accountant that he believes that we can have the Income Tax Child Allowance for Jeremy since the time that he came to us on 10th August, 1967. He says in his letter that, "... the Act states quite clearly that such allowance is due for any trial period during which the child is maintained and during which the adoptive parent has custody of it prior to the issue of the adoption certificate... assuming that Jeremy's legal parents have not made a claim for child allowance."

With such confusion, it remains to be seen if we do get the Income Tax allowance.

On the same day, I heard from the head branch Family Association in Newcastle, saying that they were glad to hear about Jeremy, and would I send them my Family Allowances book! It came back amended so that I now had a Family Allowance for Jeremy, back-dated to the time that the foster payments ceased.

The Court papers were returned from the Society, most clearly filled in and explained. There were the Application forms, Jeremy's birth certificate, the mother's consent form, marriage certificate,

This embodies something fundamental – a child with a grown-up behind them, standing firm

Jeremy's blood test results and baptism certificate. I already had the medical certificates which now had to be filled in and returned with our marriage certificate to the County Court with a fee of £1 before a date could be given for the Hearing.

The mother had signed the legal adoption form, her address was shown, and it showed that she had now married. It seemed to me unnecessary that her address had to be given for it could make her life and marriage feel just a little less secure.

When Matthew looked through the documents, he reacted in

exactly the same way, and he too wished that he did not see the address, for he often drives through the town on business. Curiously enough we both felt that we wanted to tell her how beautiful her son is, and that it is to her that he belongs. But we did not allow ourselves to look long at the address, so that it made only a small impact on us, and we did not remember it for more than a moment. However, it seemed quite wrong that we should be given her address.

We had our medicals and were all found again to be fully alive and likely to remain so. We escaped the fees, just because of the benevolence of a kind doctor.

By now we should have logged up nearly another seventeen pounds of payments for the medicals, the court fee, postage, registration of documents and telephone calls. It looks as though adoption is a costly business! We were spared most of this because of the kindness of our doctors who gave their professional services free. It is curious that ante-natal care is free under the National Health Service and ante-adoption medicals are outside the service and must be paid for privately.

The forms were lodged with the Court and the £1 fee was paid. Now we just had to wait for the Court to notify us of the date of the Hearing. How I begrudged having to pay that £1. It seemed so parsimonious for the State to extract that mean sum from us.

We were given the date for the Court Hearing. This was to be almost two and a half months hence, and we were to come to the Court with the child.

It was long past the time that I felt Jeremy and the other children should still be made conscious of all this business, and I did not think it would be good for him to miss school and attend the Court at his age. His mother was married. She did not want her child. The "Infant" as the Court office called our Jeremy, was a thinking, noticing and talkative six year old school boy, and a boy too old to be messed about any longer. I did not want Jeremy to go to the Court with us and said this to the Clerk who took my application, a pleasant and friendly young man.

"You stand the chance that the Judge will refuse to grant an adoption order if you do not bring the child," he said.

Oh, the blackmail. This judge must be a formidable being indeed! I had never met a judge in real life, and wondered how we should find him. Was he real, living flesh and blood I wondered?

How very, very glad we were going to be when it was all "fait accompli", with all the upheaval behind us. I longed for the time when we would have no more visits from the Child Care Officers, scrutinising us so delicately, which always made me self-conscious, ('phenomenon behave differently when they are observed', once said an eminence, once upon a time!) and I longed for the time when no more reports would be written about me, my precious brood and the state of us all and our home.

The Council Child Care Officer came again, and surprised me with how much she seemed to know about our family. She was adamant that Jeremy must go to Court. She also said that the majority of adoptions are not babies which, frankly, I did not believe. Oh, how the great body of Civil Servants in our top heavy Welfare State seem to feel the power in their hands. One wonders if to them everyone else except Civil Servants seems inadequate. And yet, all of them are maintained by all those of us who comprise the rest!

She told me that the Court procedure would be quite informal, with all the prospective parents and the children waiting in the Court. Each family would be summoned into the Judge's private room, where he would see us wearing no wig or gown. But Jeremy had to understand why we were going to Court, so that he could answer intelligently whatever the judge said to him.

She promised to phone me the day before going to Court to remind me. I am so absent-minded and this was one occasion it just never would do to forget! Illness, parturition, and business emergencies they were used to, but not surely simple amnesia! I was assured that in most adoptive families this was such an important day that many families celebrate adoption day as a second birthday! To us it would be just another milestone in a rich family life, a milestone of joy only because it would mean that once again we were on our own, to bring up our children as we wished without outside interference.

Nothing else, I thought, would change.

2

Both Jeremy's Godfathers sent him lovely books for Christmas; one was a very nice Bible, in the Revised Standard Version, a gift to be greatly treasured, and we were delighted with it.

Amami night was often a joyous occasion, with five heads of hair to be trimmed and washed and five young bodies bathed in quick succession. There was one short fair hair plus fringe, one short black hair, one long and thick brown hair!

I used to start off by lying the child on the bottom of a shallow bath to wet the hair, them sit them up while shampooing it. Down again to lie them flat on the bottom to rinse the head thoroughly, followed by another rinse lying on the bottom of the bath the other way round, to use the clear water at the other end of the bath.

Then, and only then, did the little body get bathed and dried and popped into their 'jamas to run downstairs to dry their hair by the gas fire, while it was touched and fingered endlessly by a much fussing Mum, trying to coax curls and waves where none exist!

"Did I always speak this language?" asked Jeremy one evening while I was combing his hair after a bath. Other children often asked if he was born in India or Africa and I suppose this had prompted the question. "Yes, you always spoke English, because you were born in this country," I said "but when you were little, you couldn't speak as well as you do now, of course."

"I suppose when I was a baby I said Mum-mum-mum, and then I started to say Mummy properly when I got bigger."

"Yes, that's how it is with babies," I said. I don't think that he would ever realise consciously that his little heart was nearly broken as a motherless baby, raised in a nursery, or that there wasn't any of that wonderful Mum-mum-mum, Dad-dad-dad phase of talking for him; no Mummy's eyes to look into, or face to feel, or breast to fondle for him, but now he has a mother and a father and I think it is alright. Time only would tell if the years spent in the nursery had done irreversible damage to his personality, or if he was resilient enough to have bounced through this adversity.

Folk occasionally asked if I felt the same about Jeremy as I did about the other children. I loved him, and often felt quite the same about him as all the other children, but I sometimes felt that we were less emotionally involved with each other than I was with the others (it was easier to be firmer with Jeremy.) This I believed was due to my not knowing him properly until he was a young boy of nearly four years old, whereas the others I had known as newborn babies, dependent on me for their every need. Part of this feeling was undoubtedly due to the knowledge, kept very, very far to the back of my mind but always there never to be forgotten, that until the child was legally adopted, he could always be taken away from us, with the Law as it stands at present. One must protect oneself against this contingency, for unlikely as it is to happen, the possibility is always there and must be borne in mind.

In one area I still did not feel quite the same. When the others were naughty, I had no compunction in spanking them, and felt they deserved it! But when I punished Jeremy I usually felt awful and long after he had recovered my conscience still felt leaden. Still lurking somewhere was the notion that I ought to be nice to him. (I hoped that this would change after the adoption was legalised but why it should, I didn't know.)

The thing I regretted most for both of us was the lack of his babyhood spent together with those endearing photographs of us cuddling yet another most beautiful baby in the world. I should have liked so much to have known him then. In many ways my love for him is like my love for Matthew – both of them came into my life half-way along the road, and it is a different love from that of the 'born' children. But none the less valid.

With his delightful warm personality, I also regretted that I have never had him on his own for long periods but only for a few brief, delightful days when we contrived to be alone together, for all sorts of obscure reasons. He was so nice and the competitive, aggressive atmosphere of a vigorous family seemed unsuitable for his soft, generous nature. But it is a competitive, tough world outside too, and perhaps this is a better preparation for later on.

We have noticed lately that he has developed a lovely singing voice and often little songs come tunefully from his darkened bedroom late into the night, to ring through the quietening house. But how often I wish he weren't troubled with his chest which means that staying with friends and holidays would always be difficult, and which can never be forgotten. He stays well now so long as he does postural drainage and coughing each morning to clear the catarrh from his chest and uses his spinhaler to reduce the allergic reaction. But I have to be on guard over his chest all the time, to see that in a gay moment he doesn't crawl into the box of dressing-up clothes or some other dusty corner or roll in the feathery eiderdowns with the other children.

He is tall and slim for his age and friends have said that he is handsome. He talks really clearly now with great understanding and interest and it seems that the days of him stammering, which lasted for only a very short while, have passed away for good. They had said at the nursery that every time he stopped wetting the bed, he started to stammer. Now he does not ever wet the bed and there is no trace of a speech defect, so I am very, very glad for him, and us too, on both counts.

He is an alive and happy little boy though he hates having to do what he doesn't want to do and occasionally sulks a bit when I coerce him into submission, but that's surely fair enough!

I sometimes wondered if he had also a touch of bronchiectasis, as he often produced a little thick phlegm when he did his 'tipping'. But no doctor had ever put down even bronchitis on the medical forms. Clearly it is such a common complaint that they consider it to be of no importance. Curiously enough though, there was no history of chronic chest trouble while Jeremy was at the nursery, though I was told that he had bronchitis as a baby, but institutions are said to have less dust than ordinary households with carpets rarely used and linen changed more often. Jeremy was wet at night in those days too, which meant clean sheets daily and feather pillows and eiderdowns were of course not used for the children in case they smothered themselves.

Though I have always deplored comparisons made between children, it was impossible not to notice that when Jeremy came to us at the age of three years eight months he was behind Louise who was just two years old in his general development. Again this never showed while he was in the sheltered environment of the nursery. Now he is six years old and Louise is four and a quarter, and Jeremy is so very much ahead of Louise in development – certainly the two years of the age gap, which is as it should be. Jeremy's "postural drainage" to give it the official title or "tipping" as it is called, consisted of leaning him over the side of his bed with his head on the cleaned floor, so that his hips were higher than his head, and while in the position, he coughed hard and repeatedly, and spat any mucus into a jam jar containing a little Milton. I kept this up for between twenty minutes and one hour, depending on how clear his chest seemed to be. This way he kept quite clear of coughs and bronchitis, and could run and play games without getting breathless or wheezy. He later learned to do his "tipping" standing on his hands and head against the wall! Windows were always open for all this.

I never mentioned how I had also treated Jeremy's knock knees, and which corrected on one year with this regime. The first thing was to insist that he always stood with his feet together, so that the weight was evenly on the knees and not, as with the feet apart continually increasing the deformity. Gradually he learned to push his knees back until they were straight.

Exercises nightly consisted of sitting cross-legged and getting up into standing, still with the feet crossed and me holding both his hands to help him up, down, later changing to put the other foot in front.

Standing feet together – bend knees forward, and push back together to straighten. Hold the child's hands as they cannot balance with their feet together and knees straight while they have got knock knees!

I also used to lie the child down occasionally on his back and hold the ankles together with my left hand and put my right hand gently on the slightly bent knees and press them straight. You may need to put a soft article between the ankles so that they don't hurt too much when they press together.

One spoonful of cod liver oil daily (or some form of Vitamin A and D, if you cannot stomach this natural food!). Follow with a spoonful of honey!

Good shoes always.

How time marches on. Jeremy came home tonight saying that there were Chinese, Japanese and dirty knees in his class at school: that old whiskery one was back again after all these years from the next generation of school boys. It was all so thrilling and so difficult to look really surprised!

3

We still have great pleasure in the hens, who have laid us 330 glorious big brown eggs in the first five months we have had them, eggs richer and more flavoursome than ever the best so called 'free range' eggs sold in the shops.

It is half way through the winter now, and the hens lay only six or seven eggs in any week during these dull grey days, but they look very well and lively. They have free access to the whole garden and a small pond and I still feed them all the household scraps from our family each day plus those bits I can glean from neighbours and local friends who will bother, and a big cupful of grain to which is added a little cod liver oil and some powdered seaweed given me by the vet. This followed a spell of 'pecking' that they inflicted one poor hen's back, due, he said to a dietary or metabolic deficiency. This cost me 10/– making the total cost of the hens plus food (but not the hen house and wire which we used to start them off with) up to £10 so far. So, all being well, after about another three months, we should be getting all our eggs almost free. But once bitten twice shy over one thing, we always shut the hen house each night so that the prowling foxes which are known to visit even the town will not devour our most productive pets.

We had a most joyful Christmas – I think the best ever for us, perhaps because the children are getting older. It was almost too much for them to wait for their parents, poor things, until after we had visited Great Granny in hospital en famille on Christmas morning, and then been to Church – taking up the whole pew next to the glittering tinsled tree to their great delight!

Then Granny and Grandpa joined us for the very best moment of the year – the opening of presents, so gaily wrapped and dotted in piles all around the room. The gifts were so simple really, yet the children had such charm as they opened them, feeling genuine joy when we managed to give them the things they wanted. New mittens for everyone, a new flannel and comb each in the child's own colour – Jackie's was blue, Peter's green, Rosemary's yellow, Jeremy's mauve and Louise's was pink, and they all have toothbrushes, mugs and towels in the same colours, which works very well and avoids confusion. Daddy and I have black and brown.

Jackie's great joy was her first ever chemistry set and she spent the rest of Christmas pouring over the instructions on the kitchen table, the smell of meths pervading the house, while she made invisible ink, crystals, and that recurring offender, bad egg gas!

Peter's day was made by the discovery of a long awaited track suit, which he then proceeded to wear day and night until school started, when at last it was relegated to the football field.

Louise got her first beautiful very own dolly, and felt very happy indeed to be a real "Mum" at last, while Rosemary's parcel opening was undoubtedly made by the discovery of a huge bag of baby oranges, which were hastily added as a make-weight by Matthew on Christmas Eve, when it appeared that her pile was much smaller than the others. She promptly squatted down behind an arm chair and ate the lot I think, and then later proceeded to knit solidly through Christmas – that very first so tantalising a scarf for teddy in yellow wool on tiny yellow needles, which of course ended up looking more holey than real, in spite of endless noble rescue attempts by Granny.

Jeremy was thrilled too with his pile, it seemed so full of the things which delighted him. At last his very own towel, a motor boat, an old fashioned car, more Bilo-fix to add to his collection and his first ever game called Mousey-Mousey, a new game to all of us, and a marvellous success for children and grown-ups of all ages. There were simple pendants for the girls, ties for the boys – flowery ones too, and chocolate to eat, a huge great bar each and for once no-one nagging them not to eat it!

We changed our routine for the first time this year, and offered just cheese and biscuits, fruit, nuts and chocolate for lunch with a candle light dinner about 5.30 p.m.

It was so very beautiful. The orange gold curtains were drawn and the soft candle light glowed gently upon everything – making the newly polished cutlery and the glass and silver glisten radiantly on the white tablecloth decorated with red streamers and red napkins. In front of each place was a tiny table decoration consisting of a baby orange holding a lighted candle, and decorated with a tiny paper doily, covering a circle of red paper serviette.

We came across one innovation this year which gave us all a lot of fun. It was the creation of some exceedingly festive headgear – edible hats – made from rice paper, icing, sweeties, nuts, chocolate, raisins, shreds of carrot, lollipops, liquorice shoe laces and much more, and the effect was the most amusing creations which really caught everyone's fancy, as they nibbled away later at their titfers. I think they really liked wearing hats for once!

My Christmas was made by a love letter from Peter which told me how much he loved me. "I was 500 and pussy was 490" it said and for me to get a higher rating than the cat was indeed a compliment. I shall be sorry when this blissful love affair ends.

The children don't know what I have written through all these years, but it came out one supper time that the story might be a bit loaded in my favour. They say that I have not emphasised enough the bad sides of my own character which seem to emerge alas far too often in my role as a Mother. So the children volunteered to write a child's eye view as they saw things after one particularly bad day! Jeremy and Louise can't write yet so they had to draw.

I remember when Rosemary started school, her first teacher had a face that was paralysed on one side, so in all the drawings the face drooped lopsidedly. Then we moved an she went to a school where the teacher managed to support a light growth of moustache and beard – and that was even more embarrassing; all the drawings had whiskers growing in the appropriate places.

Jackie and Peter had to be persuaded to write their contributions legibly – Rosemary needed no encouragement – though her phonetic spelling would no doubt amaze even Sir Isaac Pitman himself.

I wonder if Jeremy's drawing of me with no body at all has great significance? Perhaps he just forgot to put it in!

Inspired by Rosemary's gallant attempts with the needles, I have been encouraged once again to start knitting a jersey for little Louise – only being so slow I had better make if for Peter's size, then it should fit my tiniest girlie.

I have been shown a most excellent way of casting on which leaves no tight edge to tear or fray away, and looks prettier and softer:

With needles two sizes bigger than stated and using contrasting wool, cast on half the number of stitches stated.

Using correct wool, knit in stocking stitch about six rows.

Then using correct needle, pick up loops of correct colour.

With other correct needle, take stitches off alternate needles in knit 1, purl 1.

Check number of stitches with pattern and unpick contrasting colour completely.

Though this method is a little slower than the conventional way, it seems a better way for the children's garments, and indeed all knitting should pay off with less mending later on.

A flurry of white arrived silently one night, and we awoke in the morning to find a covering of snow everywhere, happily while the Christmas holidays were still with us, and this really inspired Jackie and Peter to make their first sledges themselves, with Matthew's expert help at strategic moments. By the next day, they were finished enough to go skimming over the snowy slopes of a nearby park. It was one of those days that makes people feel that they are in Switzerland, with the sun shining deeply in an orange and pink dusking sky, and the trees of the park looking majestic and strong against the white snow. It was one of those great times for the children and one of those days that makes a mother's heart glow as I watched all my five radiant children clutching each other tightly as they went down the steep, bumpy hillside together with both toboggans roped to form one, trying not to loose the crew overboard on the frenzied journey.

My little journey impressed me greatly too. No whining about pulling up sledges back to take-off point, or fear to go alone head first. (I recalled how to start with two winters ago, his back was so stiff that it seemed difficult for him to lie on his tummy on the sledge and look ahead!) But, man alive – once I saw him speeding down on his tummy with eleven year old Jackie lying flat on top of him. And he is still alive to tell the tale!

He has grown so manful latterly and he and Peter sometimes spend long times together, as after the tobogganing when I let them walk back home alone together, pulling their sledges behind them. I was glad when they got home safely for I wondered what would happen if Jeremy ever had an accident, even though I considered it perfectly safe. Never, I felt sure, would it then be considered wise that I thought it good for them to have this sort of responsibility for their character development. Because he was technically a 'foster' child, I knew that I was always at risk. What would the reaction have been if it had been Jeremy and not Louise who had cut his artery and he had died because I was in the garden perhaps and not instantly on hand to arrest the bleeding?

These things put a foster parent in a most invidious and unenviable position; a position always of risk if anything should go wrong with the child, or any tragedy occurs. Yet to allow a child to grow up to full manhood one has to take reasonable risks to allow them to try out themselves and the world about them, to gain self-confidence and to do the 'big' things of life.

We now heard from the Accountant concerning the Income Tax Allowance Claim for Jeremy. It seems that once again the great bureaucratic machine prefers not to give a definite answer even to a situation that was absolutely concrete.

The letter as from H.M. Inspector of Taxes stated… "In the circumstances, I suggest that the question of Child Allowance be left in abeyance until… the adoption is finalised. I should then like to see the certified copy of entry in the Adopted Children's Register, and at the same time any other documents which have been exchanged between the… Society and Mr. Macdonald, so that I can consider the question of any allowance for earlier years."

After a talk with our Society Child Care Officer, Matthew phoned the Tax Office himself and dealt directly with the lady H.M. Inspector in person, who said on the phone that if we could prove that we had taken Jeremy for adoption, not for fostering, then the allowance could be paid. We obtained a letter from the Society to that effect and Matthew phoned the Tax Office one weekday afternoon at 4.40 p.m. to find that everyone had already gone home. So next day, he then drove right over to the Tax Office to find that the clerk dealing with his application had left that job.

He was now dealt with by a young man who heard the full story, read the Society's letter and said that he felt that the claim was justified and his Tax Inspector agreed. In discussion, however, it appeared that the law was not entirely clear. It stated that if an allowance which was insufficient in the eyes of the Inspector had been paid to the prospective adoptive parents, a claim would be justified. If the fostering allowance was deemed by him to be obviously sufficient to cover the cost of looking after the child, it was still left to his discretion.

A claim that could be met at the Inspector's discretion, but here the law stated that no allowance need be paid prior to the three months before the adoption. One can only assume that the law was made for adopting babies only!

We did not feel the information we got to be really reliable. It seems that if the adoptive or foster parents believe that no tax allowance is being claimed for the child by the natural parents, it is well worth at least trying to get a tax allowance prior to the legal adoption. Not that it will make all the difference in the world. We got £94 for the two years tax, back-dated to the April before Jeremy came to us. We were absolutely overjoyed though to have accomplished it, and used part of it to buy, at long last, a desperately needed sewing machine.

We pay tax at the Standard Rate. Financially, it appears that fostering is a better bet than adoption, even with the abysmal rates of fostering, for payment of family allowances plus the tax allowances comes to only a very small amount when compared to the cost of keeping the child.

It is a morbid thought for the boys and girls left in the nurseries and children's homes. In these highly inflationary days, how are we going to afford to get them out, for even with the best will in the world NO-ONE can keep a child in England for the few pounds offered.

How can taxation laws be so merciless in its effect on the children?

How very dearly I should like to know just how many children over about two years old, who are placed for adoption, still stay in institutions in our country today.

4

The Society Child Care Officer came again and her visit was, as always, a pleasure. She told me, in passing, of one gorgeous little Anglo-Chinese boy of three years old who was still awaiting adoption in one of the Society's nurseries. He had straight black hair, nice eyes, and lovely rosy cheeks, she said, and only a touch of the oriental look and yet still he was unwanted. Oh, how tempted one feels!

Later, I went up to this nursery with a friend and spent an hour being taken round and talking to the Matron, the Sister and the children. There were seventeen children, fourteen of whom were for adoption and nine of whom were coloured. Only three were young babies.

We saw the little Anglo-Chinese boy, who was indeed a fine child called Keith, actually four years old, and so slightly oriental that I doubt that I would have noticed if I had not been told.

Jamie was the child who won my heart completely. An absolute poppet of a most beautiful Anglo-Jamaican mixture with English features, lightly brown skin, fair and slightly curly hair, and the most gorgeous outgoing personality. He too was four years old.

Then among this little band of older children were two very sweet Anglo-West Indian children of three years old, with warm soft natures, and both of whom spoke only very indistinctly. There were also two fair haired English boys of four and three with whom we made poor contact. I did not hear them speak and they seemed pale and a little withdrawn. We learned that some senior staff had left at Christmas and this had upset these children who were now wetting the beds even during short rest periods, as their tender emotions were disturbed while they started to get to know the new people in charge of them. Even with the small "family" groupings in operation in the nursery, the staff must sometimes change, making an upheaval in the young lives and making it so unlike a real family, where Mummy and Daddy at least stay constant.

Unfortunately, all the toddlers between one and three years old were out on a walk when we called, so we were only able to see the older children and the babies, two of whom were soon going for adoption and one of whom was a beautiful blind Indian babe of thirteen months. She was developing much too slowly, and she above all I felt, needed the loving care of one constant, continuous foster parent, who could devote herself to this work – a modern Anne Sullivan who released Helen Keller from her prison. This babe was physically much soft in her musculature, and was still unable to sit up or roll over. Of course, she probably did not realise that everyone else walks or sits and needed constant care by one skilful and devoted person to be her eyes for her before too much time was lost. She was not as curious as I would have expected for that age, for even without eyes in a normal environment, I would have expected her little hands to be into everything and exploring the marvellous world. But in a nursery, the one single Mother stimulus is missing. How surely Helen Keller would have gone completely mad if she had been continually handled by a stream of different people with different attitudes, instead of the consistency of one single person in her teacher and friend, who saved her sanity. In this babe's case, it was promised that her sight could be restored to a useful level in the future, with operations and glasses to follow, so the future was bright, but not if she was too emotionally deprived as well.

It was a wonderful visit. Surely someone, somewhere, must come forward to be Keith's new Mummy and Daddy – a Mum please must come for fine little Jamie, and please, God, will someone take little Jillie, and the others before they are too sad-hearted to be restored.

The visit did something for me. It made me tremendously glad about Jeremy. I felt more tender towards him, and it all seemed a great miracle that we had succeeded in getting him out of the nursery and into our family, when all the odds were against it.

In this nursery, it was warm and clean, playrooms abounded and they were kind, sympathetic and affectionate towards the children, and yet, it was so unlike a real home. As unlike a real home as a greenhouse is to a real garden. A sheltered environment and the most unsuitable place to produce hardy individuals, tough enough to stand up to the real rigours of life. I have a feeling that to produce adults with strong minds, bodies, spirits and emotions, one must run the gamut of many experiences as a child, while one is able to go home to a sympathetic Mother and Father, so that one is then sturdy enough to cope with the changed but not dissimilar experiences of adulthood.

There will, of course, always be many children who will need nursery care, including some of the many badly handicapped little folk, but it is for the group of children who have been placed for adoption that I feel so desperately. With no viable Mum and Dad in the background, their need for new parents is so very great.

To my joy, I have now been able to find out what happened to some of the children I talked to earlier in the story.

I hear that Nicola has been restored to her Mother.

Anita, Pippa and Stuart have been placed for adoption.

Unfortunately, I have not been able to find out what happened to Miranda. Shirley now lives in a Children's Home. Jeremy will soon be ours. I hear too that Sarah has been visited by her Mother, who hopes to have her home with her.

How thankful one feels about these little ones who have found their niche, and are now somebody's fine son or daughter. But how heavy is one's heart for little Shirley, now about six, who is still nobody's child, living in the kindly but unreal world of the Children's Home, knowing that for reasons she understands not, she has no Mum or Dad like other kids, and belongs especially to no-one.

5

One evening, we were sitting around the dining room table rather later than usual. The younger girls were both bedded earlier than usual, and Peter and Jeremy had just come back from playing football in the park, so incredibly dirty. We had managed to get the mud scraped off the palms of their hands with soap and water, to my triumph, though the faces did not fare so well. Jackie had just come in late from her drama class, to make a smaller-than-usual supper time together.

Quite out of the blue, Peter's voice piped up "I wish I had a real brother."

"But I am real," said Jeremy grinning.

We knew exactly what Peter meant and were delighted by Jeremy's sense of humour which made us laugh. I had truly tried to get a real brother for Peter, but quite unexpectedly, I had lost the recipe. I never did find it again, and so for us, this was the best alternative!

I think that over-all it was a good alternative. I used to wonder what would happen to Peter if Matthew were killed and he were left the only boy among four women, all having puberties or the menopause in a few years, a formidable thought! Now there were two of them and that made three with Matthew. It was a much healthier situation.

Matthew remarked the other day that he thought that Peter was a bit "smelly" and wondered if he were a bit below par. I had noticed it too, but I had bathed and hair-washed him the night before and he looked well and rosy, and so I was a bit perplexed until the next day when I was putting clean clothes away in his drawers. There, wrapped in polythene and hiding discreetly among his clothes was the ripest, stinkiest cheese I have ever seen. It was almost walking and had obviously been there since Christmas, which was now a long time ago, perfuming all his clothes with a most distinguished pong. No wonder he smelled!

The citrus fruits are absolutely gorgeous during the earliest months of the year, and so I took the opportunity to replenish my depleted stocks once again with jars of soft flavoured marmalade that are made from mixed citrus fruits and can actually be made almost any time of the year :

1 large grapefruit
2 (sweet) oranges
2 large lemons

4 pints water
4 ½ 1bs. demerara sugar
Scrub and dry the fruit, squeeze out the juice, and cut skins into thin slices with a sharp knife. Tie pips into a muslin bag, put juice into a jug.

Soak the skins in 4 pints of water overnight (with the pips in a muslin bag).

Simmer skins and pips for 1 ½ hours.

Remove pips. Add juice and sugar. Stir until dissolved. Boil until marmalade sets, stirring continuously. (To test for a set, put a little onto a plate and leave to cool. When cool, it will be a little solid and wrinkle when pushed with the finger. Dot and cover.

This will make about 8 1bs. of marmalade of a delicious flavour, and if cooked gently of a light colour, at a cost of about 1/6d. per jar.

One morning, "Fred" called collecting money for the Salvation Army. We had got to know him a little after his visit last year and we found him an interesting visitor and one with such a story to tell.

To look at him, one would not notice him in a crowd. He is a cook in an Old People's Home, not very tall, dark or handsome, but one of those people who are the backbone of our country. He spends every minute of his spare time bringing joy working for the "Army" in a million different ways and for the Lord Jesus, whom he clearly loves a lot. With his three weeks holiday this year, he has spent one week tramping from door to door collecting funds for the "Army", one week he will take twenty-two old people to Torquay for a holiday, and one week he and his wife will go away together, which for a man with two coronaries to his record is quite something.

When he called, he was so tired and glad of a cup of coffee and a snack for he trekked this hilly district each day from 9 a.m. to 4 p.m. without a break, trying to encourage people to pop something into those little envelopes. But it was his wartime story that really thrilled me. He was a prisoner of war, and early on in his captivity, he asked if he might hold a service in the camp for the inmates. This was agreed and a small notice was put on a wall inviting the prisoners to that first meeting. Two thousand came to hear this man preach, many of differing faiths or of none. He is not an educated man, nor a clergyman, but just an ordinary Fred of this world with only one qualification – he had given his life to Jesus Christ, and this was something he could do for him, and the services continued – just like in the days of the early Church when quite ordinary folk filled with the Spirit of God preached to these huge crowds, using no previous advertising campaigns or modern crowd gathering techniques to boost their audiences. Folk just wanted to hear about a living God from someone who knew.

His other camp activities included the escape committee, on which they were pledged not to try to escape themselves, but to devote themselves to helping others to escape, and the entertainments committee, which seemed to get up to many a prank to keep the soldiers amused.

Peter was at home when he called and he promised to send him a record of a Salvation Army beat group, which tours all around the country bringing the Christian news in the joyous style of the modern idiom.

One night, I dreamed that we'd had the Court Hearing; while we waited, in the dream, one very elderly lady sat on a bench nursing a new baby, and said warmly how much she loved her daughter. Clearly she had adopted the unmarried mother and the baby. (A marvellous idea!) Another group were standing round admiring another mother's baby – clearly a young polar bear! (I was sure they were unaware that those furry paws did not belong to a real human baby!) Then the dream ended. They say that dreams are prophetic, but surely no-one was really going to adopt a polar bear at our Court Hearing?

"When I am a Mummy, I am not going to have any children," announced Louise, one night. I was surprised for she liked babies. "Well then, I will just have girls. Some children get adopted, don't they Mummy, when their Mummy and Daddy don't like them anymore, like Jeremy did. His Mummy did not like him," she went on.

"Well, it wasn't quite like that," I replied "for his Mummy did like him, but she was not married and had no money to look after him, and so she sadly had to ask the nursery to find another Mummy and Daddy who were married to look after him." I hoped that I had put the situation fairly, and dispelled any possible idea that she too might be sent away to be adopted too. What a nightmarish thought. She loves me tremendously at the moment, so no wonder she is devastated when I am cross with her if such a thought had ever occurred to her.

Only once have I heard some children singing that no-one wanted Jeremy. Once too, someone lightheartedly said that we should sell Jeremy when it seemed inconvenient to have him, but another child shut it up instantly.

The night before our real life Court Hearing, I talked to Jeremy alone and told him what we were going to do the following morning. We were going to the Court to see a man called a Judge, who would give us a paper top say that Jeremy was our dear adopted boy for always, and would write it down in the big adoption book in London, so that the Government would know all about it.

Then we once again went through the details of why he was adopted, as I had been told I must do. "Do you know why you were adopted Jeremy?"

"Yes, because the mother was not married and she could not look after me," he said. It no longer meant anything to him – he had a mother. I was his mother.

"Will you say that to the Judge in the morning, if he asks you?" I said.

"If I can remember," he smiled doubtfully.

The following morning, the other children went off to school, and I bathed our young hero, and washed his dark locks, and brushed his teeth as never before. He positively shone and glowed with the extra attention lavished on his especially this morning, and to have Matthew and I both together to himself alone was indeed an occasion. It was lovely.

We had to be there by 10.15 – a very early appointment indeed for me these days! It was a bright, clear, sunny morning, with a smell of spring in the air, and we all had on our best bib and tuckers. I hid under my beautiful big red cowboy hat that I bought in the Sales, and since someone said I looked elegant – I felt elegant.

We walked through the forbidding doors and up the stairs to the Courtroom itself, where we were to wait. It was a County Court, where civil cases of divorce and bankruptcy were heard, a light cheerful room in modern style, so different from the gloomy old dark brown Court rooms one imagines are the norm. Our Local Authority Child Care Officer was waiting for us. Gradually the room filled up with about eight families; there were a lot of people and many babies and children.

A man with a gentle, smiling face came in. "Who is that?" I asked. It was the Clerk of the Court. He called the first family to go in. We were the third family.

We went through the door to the Judge's private room. Behind a huge desk sat a big, elderly man; in front of him, spaced well apart, were about six grey chairs. "Sit yourselves down," he said.

"Good morning," said Matthew.

He replied, "Good morning."

We sat down. Matthew, myself, Jeremy and the Child Care Officer, all well apart, facing the Judge.

"Do you understand that if I grant an adoption order, it is absolutely irreversible? The child will be yours for ever and ever," said the Judge.

"Yes, we do," said Matthew and I.

He turned to the Child Care Officer. Are you satisfied with this case?" he asked.

"Yes, I am," she replied.

"Do you realise that in adopting this child, there will be many difficulties later in life?" he went on depressingly.

"There are always difficulties," replied Matthew.

"Yes, but there will be special difficulties."

I felt gloomy. He had no aura that one sometimes perceives in the presence of the great. He had not smiled yet.

"What do the other children think of having a new brother?" he asked.

"Nothing now," replied Matthew. "Nothing now" he reiterated.

"Do you know if he has had all his immunisations?" he went on.

I replied coldly that he'd had them all as a baby.

"Does he know why he has come here this morning?" he asked.

"Yes, he does," I replied anxiously and turned to Jeremy. "Can you tell the Judge what I told you last night?"

He sat silent. He had completely forgotten! I went through it all again with him to ensure that the Judge knew that I had told it all – this was critical – it had been emphasised – he must know that he was adopted. "He really does know and understands about it, Sir."

He nodded. Silence for a moment. I felt my red face return again, and hoped that the hat hid it.

"I will sign the order."

His pen moved briefly over the bundle of papers before him, and he passed them to the Clerk of the Court who I think had been standing there at the side all the time, but I had not noticed him.

Matthew got up masterfully and walked right over to the Judge and held out his hand. "Thank you" he said, smiling, as he so often does.

At this, the Judge became a person. He smiled and shook hands with Matthew. "I think you ought to shake hands Jeremy," said Matthew, propelling Jeremy round the side of the big desk.

"Thank you," I said.

Then we were outside.

"He was nice," said Jeremy. Tears welled up inside me and down again quickly! Matthew was being very practical and marching us very fast off for a lovely hot coffee. It had actually taken six minutes in the Judge's Chamber – twenty minutes, including the waiting.

It was cold outside now, and raining, so the warn coffee was welcome. Jeremy tried out a strawberry milk shake for the first time and a huge chocolate biscuit plus a host of sugar lumps wrapped in those little cube packets, while Matthew and I chatted about the morning. The thing we both felt was that it was a great pity that in this sort of case such a formal atmosphere had to pervade, when surely this above all was a human situation. Why, oh why couldn't he have wished us all joy and happiness together as a finale, and finished up on a positive note?

Matthew had a surprise for Jeremy in the car, unknown to me. It was a most beautiful silver napkin ring for him to treasure always.

How does one end a story that has barely begun?

At last, after a long search, and a long, long wait, Jeremy was ours. I was immensely glad and very thankful to look so often at his beaming face and shining eyes, and so grateful that we had been allowed this young boy.

Yes, we did have room for one more. So far the pennies had stretched far

Enough to support us all, and our children loved Jeremy as much as they loved each other. Jeremy was a normal, lovely boy, with healthful attitudes about people and God, with no problems and no inhibitions. He feels loved and liked. He knows that parents are living people who love and quarrel and make up and go on loving, and he loves us too.

I think that we were in time 'to mend his broken heart' but I will tell you this when Jeremy is grown up. I think his loss may have turned to a glorious gain, for as things had turned out well for him, it is possible that his experiences may have enriched him more than if he had trodden a smoother path.

Perhaps I can do no more than say, with Rudyard Kipling :

If you can keep your head when all about you
Are losing theirs and blaming it on you,
If you can trust yourself when all men doubt you,
But make allowance for their doubting too;
If you can wait and not be tired by waiting,
Or being lied about, don't deal in lies,
Or being hated, don't give way to hating,
And yet don't look too good, nor talk too wise:

If you can dream – and not make dreams your master;
If you can think – and not make thoughts your aim;
If you can meet with Triumph and Disaster
And treat those two impostors just the same;
If you can bear to hear the truth you've spoken
Twisted by knaves to make a trap for fools,
Or watch the things you your life to, broken,
And stoop and build 'em up with worn-out tools:

If you can make one heap of all your winnings
And risk it one turn of pitch-and-toss,
And lose, and start again at your beginnings

And never breathe a word about your loss;
If you can force your heart and nerve and sinew
To serve your turn long after they are gone,
And so hold on when there is nothing in you
Except the Will which says to them: "Hold on!"

If you can talk with crowds and keep your virtue
Or walk with Kings – nor lose the common touch,
If neither foes nor loving friends can hurt you,
If all men count with you, but none too much;
If you can fill the unforgiving minute
With sixty seconds' worth of distance run,
Yours is the Earth and everything that's in it,
And – which is more – you'll be a Man, my son!

It was the last day of term, and I peeped round the classroom door.

"Your mum's here, Jeremy," shouted one of the children.

"Hi, Mum." Two smiling eyes turned to face me. And a warm hand slipped into my palm…